Why We Homeschool

Why We Homeschool
The Meaning and Significance
of Christian Education

Adam T. Calvert

WIPF & STOCK · Eugene, Oregon

WHY WE HOMESCHOOL
The Meaning and Significance of Christian Education

Copyright © 2018 Adam T. Calvert. All rights reserved. Except for brief quotations in critical publications or reviews, no part of this book may be reproduced in any manner without prior written permission from the publisher. Write: Permissions, Wipf and Stock Publishers, 199 W. 8th Ave., Suite 3, Eugene, OR 97401.

Wipf & Stock
An Imprint of Wipf and Stock Publishers
199 W. 8th Ave., Suite 3
Eugene, OR 97401

www.wipfandstock.com

PAPERBACK ISBN: 978-1-5326-5590-6
HARDCOVER ISBN: 978-1-5326-5591-3
EBOOK ISBN: 978-1-5326-5592-0

Manufactured in the U.S.A.   07/18/18

Scripture quotations are from the ESV® Bible (The Holy Bible, English Standard Version®), copyright © 2001 by Crossway, a publishing ministry of Good News Publishers. Used by permission. All rights reserved.

To Mary, my helpmate and partner in loving and pursuing our Lord and Savior Jesus Christ—and in raising our children to be his disciples.

> *"Her children rise up and call her blessed;*
> *her husband also, and he praises her:*
> *'Many women have done excellently,*
> *but you surpass them all.'"*
>
> —PROVERBS 21:28-29

To Lilianna Joelle, Olivia Joy, and Clara Jane, the joy and cheer of my heart. May you always know the love our Lord has for you, and that the love your mother and I have for you is second in line. And may our Lord keep you grounded in his word throughout your lives.

> *"I have no greater joy than to hear*
> *that my children are walking in the truth."*
>
> —3 JOHN 1:4

Contents

Preface | ix

Introduction: Christian Education | 1

Section 1: The Meaning of Christian Education | 9

Chapter 1: Christ: The Foundation, Means, and Goal of All Knowledge | 11

Chapter 2: Parents: The Stewards of Discipleship | 18

Chapter 3: Children: The Foremost Disciples of the Great Commission | 30

Section 2: The Significance of Christian Education | 41

Chapter 4: Language Arts | 45

Chapter 5: Mathematics | 53

Chapter 6: Natural Sciences | 59

Chapter 7: Social Sciences | 62

Chapter 8: Creative Arts | 68

Chapter 9: Conclusion | 72

Appendix 1: How Our Children Will Develop Socially | 75

Appendix 2: Homeschooling Versus Private Christian Schooling | 78

Appendix 3: A Special Note to My Friends Involved in Government Schools | 81

Bibliography | 87

Preface

WHY THIS BOOK?

There are several informative and well-written works on the topic of homeschooling and Christian education. So why write another one? The reason is pretty simple. This book has a particular audience that isn't usually addressed in the other books. And I think it would do well to have a book just for them.

While this work is not *primarily* for those who are already interested in the subject of Christian education or homeschooling, my hope is that it would be beneficial for them as well. However, the primary audience for this book are my Christian brothers and sisters (whether friends, family, or strangers) who are asking those of us who *do* homeschool our kids, why we do it.

What I have found in my discussions, when the topic of homeschooling comes up, is that there often seem to be various assumptions as to why we homeschool our children, which are simply wrong, or, at best, inadequate. Yes, the government schools have bullies; yes, the government schools might be bigger targets for armed shootings; and yes, the government schools (even the ones in good school districts) have kids or teachers who will teach our children language or experiences that we would rather them not learn that early in life (or at all).

And while all those things are true and good reasons to educate our children at home, even if those problems were corrected, we—and many other parents—would still be committed to homeschooling our children.

PREFACE

Why?

The purpose of this book is to answer that question. In my experience, anytime the topic of education comes up, and I disclose that my wife and I are homeschooling our children, after the inevitable reluctant nod of hesitant affirmation (even from family members and friends—"Oh . . . Okay . . . ?"), it'd be nice to actually give them solid reasons to answer the primary question that seems to be ever nagging them: "Why don't you just send your kids to public school?"[1] Usually a follow-up question regarding homeschooling specifically is: "How will they develop socially without interaction with other kids?"

The short answers to these questions are: (1) because we want our children to be disciples of Jesus Christ rather than disciples of the state, and (2) our children *will* have interaction with other kids. However, we believe they will develop better socially, and in a much healthier environment, if *we* encourage, promote, and oversee their social interactions (not just with children but also with adults), than if we let them learn most of their social interactions from their peers (who are just as naive and/or destructive in their childish state).

But you can't just give those short answers to people. Reading it has possibly already put many on the defensive. So, again, that is why I'm writing this book: so that I can explain in a polite, rational manner, briefly and thoroughly to whomever in the audience is willing to listen, my reasoning behind why both my wife and I, as well as many other Christian parents around the world, are personally committed to our children being educated at home from a Christian worldview.

Clearly, I cannot presume to speak on behalf of the entire homeschooling community (nor would I want to). However, there are many of us throughout the world who are committed to educating our children at home from a Christian worldview. While this work is certainly about why my wife and I in particular

---

1. Though not always, often enough this question is made with an underlying air of: "I mean, after all, aren't the teachers in the public schools more qualified to teach your children than you are?"

PREFACE

homeschool our children, it's also about why *we*—collectively as those dedicated to raising up our children as disciples of Jesus Christ—homeschool our kids.

To be clear, the main focus of this book is to address the first question above: Why don't we just send our children to public—that is, government—schools? The reason for that is because the main purpose of our homeschooling is found in the contrast between Christian education and state education. How our children will develop socially can be found in Appendix A. To be sure, I'm very glad for private Christian schools, but in Appendix B you can read a brief discussion on the preference I have for homeschooling, even when private Christian schools are available.

It is necessary to make one more qualifying point. This book is not intended to shame my Christian brothers and sisters who teach or administer in government schools, nor those parents who send their children to government schools because they otherwise cannot make ends meet. This book is simply written in *defense* of *Christian education* over against the secular-humanist, state-sponsored *curriculum* that government schools would try to use to teach our children.[2] To my friends who are teachers or administrators, or parents of kids involved in the government schools, you can find a special note to you in Appendix C.

Of course, it is only right that I am up front with you that none of these thoughts came from me alone, but from several other teachers, theologians, biblical scholars, pastors, and other parents whom I was blessed to come across in my life.[3] It is a great hope of mine that in reading this, you don't see me as pompous or arrogant. If it had not been for the grace of God in my life working

---

2. The secular-humanism of the state-sponsored curriculum is the real threat that I aim to address in this book; and this work will not go into detail regarding the "taxation is theft" view of economics in education. As a side note (for those interested), I personally do not think the civil government has a Biblically legitimate role in the education of our children.

3. For a more specific but still limited list of resources on the topic of homeschooling or Christian education, that are either more thorough on the topic, or philosophical (or both), I'll direct your attention to the further resources listed in the back.

through the people and books and lectures he worked through, I would see no problem with government schools; and I would be asking those "crazy homeschooling parents" the same question(s) you may be asking us. However, I do think he has opened our eyes through those people—and used them only as a means of opening our eyes to his word and what *it* says about education in general and educating our children in particular.

I should say up front, though, that the two biggest influences on *my* mindset regarding Christian education came from chapter 1 of Cornelius Van Til's *Foundations of Christian Education*,[4] and the lecture series from Greg L. Bahnsen entitled *A Thousand Generations*.[5]

Likewise, just as none of these thoughts came from me alone, the production of this work was by no means mine alone. While I wish I could thank every person who helped me, the list would be too long. But I want to publicly thank these specific individuals who helped me directly with this work:

- First, I'd like to thank Dannah Chalupka. She was the first to edit the manuscript, and she provided a tremendous amount of corrections in grammar and syntax. Further, she provided an invaluable amount of truly helpful suggestions on flow of thought and how the reader might perceive the writing. Anything of hers I ignored was, I'm sure, by mistake. And I bear the responsibility of that.

- I'd also like to thank my good friend Neil Erickson. He likewise provided valuable input on the manuscript and how it could be improved—both in flow and in content. His insights and questions caused me to ponder a little more from the reader's perspective what objections might be made and how I might address them (or not cause them to begin with).

---

4. Berkhof, Louis and Cornelius Van Til, *Foundations of Christian Education: Addresses to Christian Teachers*, P & R; Reprint edition (December 1, 1989).

5. Bahnsen, Greg L. *A Thousand Generations*, Covenant Media Foundation; http://www.cmfnow.com/athousandgenerations.aspx.

Preface

- I must especially express my gratitude for my best friend, John Eastes. When I first met John in Sunday School several years ago, I was simultaneously inspired by his zeal for discovering God's truth in Scripture, and intimidated by his knowledge of God's word (intimidated because *I* was supposed to be the Sunday School teacher). John not only provided tremendous feedback on the content and flow of the manuscript, but he also painstakingly looked up every Bible reference throughout. He brought to my attention any of the typos I had created, and/or graciously questioned me on whether or not I needed to include certain references. I don't know of a better friend I have (obviously, outside of my wife).

- This, of course, brings me to my extreme gratitude for my wife. Mary encouraged the project and gave her unique and insightful perspective on the ideas and the ways they were presented. She did this all while continuing her daily labor of love in taking care of our house and girls. I would not be able to have completed this project without her help. And I am truly grateful for her and all she does.

While I have had such tremendous help from all of these people and others, and I thank all of them, any flaws or failures in the final product are mine alone, for which I take full responsibility.

Lastly, and most importantly, I thank my Lord and Savior Jesus Christ, who has saved me from the penalty of my sin, from my rebellion against him in my walk, and for securing an eternal redemption and promise of bliss forevermore with him. It is only because of what he has done that any truth in this work has surfaced through my bumbling and stumbling hands. To whatever degree this work has merit—to him be the glory forever and ever!

Introduction: Christian Education

"He has delivered us from the domain of darkness..."
—COLOSSIANS 1:13

ALL HUMANITY IS COMMANDED to worship God. The greatest commandment from him is to love him with all our heart, soul, mind, and strength, and to love our neighbors as ourselves (Luke 10:27; cf. Deut 6:5).

Yet man, by himself, *cannot* do this and *will not* do this. Jesus said man is depraved on the *inside*: it is *from* his evil heart that come forth the evil deeds that man does throughout his time on earth (Matt 15:19).

The apostle Paul teaches that we, by ourselves, are in rebellion against God (Rom 1:18–32), and due to our corrupt nature with which we were born (Rom 5:12; cf. Ps 51:5) do not seek for him and will not seek for him (Rom 3:10–12), cannot please him (Rom 8:7–8), that we are futile in our thinking, darkened in our understanding, and callous in our hearts (Eph 4:18–19), that we live a life of hatred through slavery to passions and pleasures (Titus 3:3), that we are in the power of Satan (2 Cor 4:3–4; 1 John 5:19), and that we are spiritually dead to all things concerning a saving knowledge of the Lord Jesus Christ (1 Cor 2:14; cf. Eph 2:1).

How then are we to love God with all our heart, soul, mind, and strength? Paul, through the work of the Holy Spirit, answers that for us too:

> Wretched man that I am! Who will deliver me from this body of death? Thanks be to God through Jesus Christ our LORD! (Rom 7:24–25)

Because of what Christ has done on the cross and through his resurrection, those who trust in him do so because they have been born again by the Spirit of God (John 3:3, 7), have been spiritually resurrected (Eph 2:1–6), are now seen as righteous in God's eyes and legally declared as such (Rom 4:5, 5:1, 8:1), and seek to live in a way that is pleasing to God (Rom 12:1–3) in *every* facet of their lives (1 Cor 10:31).

We who have fled for refuge under Jesus Christ (Heb 6:18) are righteous in our relationship to God because of what Christ has done on our behalf and not for anything we have done for ourselves (Heb 7:25, 10:14). Though we will still sin on this side of our final redemption (Rom 8:22–25; 1 John 1:8, 10), we have the glorious work of the Spirit dwindling down our desire for sin (1 John 3:9), from the moment we are born again (Titus 3:4–7) to the time we are face to face with our Lord and Savior (2 Cor 3:18).

These are the glorious truths of the gospel; and they must be at the forefront of all that we do (Eph 2:10) *and* think (1 Cor 2:16; Eph 4:22–24). It is precisely because we understand the good news of our Lord Jesus Christ (through *the Spirit's* regenerative, enabling power) that we lead our lives continually seeking to be a living sacrifice (Rom 12:1–3).

Furthermore, this life that is sanctified in Christian truth (John 17:17) affects *every* aspect of our being, including what we learn and how we learn it; that is, including our education. That Jesus Christ is Lord does not just affect our relationship with the triune God, it affects our relationship with everything in his universe. And we say again, this includes education.

Christian education is much more than beginning or ending an instructional class with prayer to the Christian God. And *any*

Introduction: Christian Education

education is much more than learning *facts*. Christian education is, plain and simple, Christian discipleship; and it encompasses all areas of life.

But before we move any further in a book on *Christian Education*, let us define these two words at the start.

Education

Education, at its root, is discipleship.

If someone says, "That man is a disciple of so-and-so," what they mean is that that man has learned and/or is learning from so-and-so. He is being taught how to think by so-and-so. He is being *educated* by so-and-so.

In other words, *to be* educated by someone is *to be* that person's disciple. There is a reason that when Jesus said a disciple is not above his teacher (Luke 6:40), translations differ on translating the Greek word for disciple as "student" or "disciple." In the Greek language there is no difference. A student is a disciple. It is someone who learns not just fact, but a whole system of thought and interpretation of fact from someone else.

Obviously, we can learn facts from someone without having a formal (or informal) discipleship with them. And when that happens we don't feel the need to say we've been educated by him. If we ask what time it is, and a nearby non-Christian reports it to us, we're not being educated by him, though he's given us a fact.

So, what makes education different from learning facts?

Education is not *simply* learning facts from a teacher, but also learning his *philosophy of fact*, or how he arrives at those facts. It's learning the facts that the teacher knows *along with* his interpretation of those facts.

For instance, when a math teacher teaches a student that 2+2=4, he is not simply teaching a fact, but a *system* of how to arrive at the knowledge of that fact. He will explain that when you have two of something and add two more, the result is that you end up with a total of four of those things. That is a fact.

Now, the teacher might not explicitly say this, but what he will teach is that the principles of mathematics are universal; that is, they apply at all places and at all times. Two plus two equals four whether we're in the US or in China, and whether we are here today or we live a thousand years from now. Two plus two does, always has, and always will equal four.[1] And that is a fact... Or is it?

It is here where the teacher's educating principles are very important. Do we know the fact that 2+2=4 at all times and all places because we ourselves have universal knowledge? Of course not. Only the Christian God, who himself is transcendent (Ps 90:2; Isa 41:21–23, 43:10–11, 46:8–11) can have that kind of knowledge.

Do we know it because we rely on the principle of induction; that is, the presumption that the future will behave like the past? And since 2+2=4 was always the case in the past, do we have reason to believe it will always be like that in the future?

Perhaps. But that just begs another question: If we know that 2+2=4 by relying on the principle of induction, how did we learn that the principle of induction is a reliable method for learning and using other facts? Did *God* reveal to us that we can rely on the principle of induction, or are we simply relying on it for pragmatic reasons, or on our own say-so, *or on the teacher's own say-so*?

Here, friends, a teacher's worldview and principles of interpreting facts comes to a very important head. And it is here, even at the beginning of 2+2=4, that a disciple is first taught to think after the thought life of his teacher. So, let us think of our children even at this point in their lives.

From what kind of teacher do we want our children to be discipled? For Jesus did not mince words when he said, "Everyone when he is fully trained will be like his teacher" (Luke 6:40). Now, it is easy at this point to throw our hands up saying, "Come on!

---

1. I was first struck by just how dependent our knowledge on God is, even for something as basic as 2+2=4, when I first read Cornelius Van Til's chapter, "Antitheses in Education," in the book *Foundations of Christian Education* (although the example he used was 2x2=4). However, if you wish to think through mathematics in particular more thoroughly from a Christian perspective, I very highly recommend Vern S. Poythress's *Redeeming Mathematics: A God-Centered Approach*.

Is it really that important to delve this deep into 2+2=4?" And of course, we think it is. But before that happens, let us consider one basic yet crucial thing when it comes not just to our education, but to every facet of our lives:

> So, whether you eat or drink, or whatever you do, do all to the glory of God. (1 Cor 10:31)

And that brings us to the *Christian* aspect of *Christian Education*.

Christian

Man is born in sin (Ps 51:5). He is corrupt in his heart and mind (Eph 4:17–18) from the very beginning (Gen 6:5, 8:21). Unless he is born again by the Holy Spirit, he will not want to glorify God. Unbelieving sinners never want to glorify the one true God (Rom 3:10–12), and unless they are converted by the Spirit of God (Titus 3:4–7) they are never able to do it actively (Rom 8:8; 1 Cor 2:14).

So, if we're commanded to love the Lord our God with our whole being, even to love him with all our *mind* (Matt 22:37), and commanded to glorify him in whatever we do (1 Cor 10:31), then certainly how we think and how we apply that thinking, how we learn and the degree to which we learn it, is something with which our Lord is concerned.

In other words, education (or discipleship) is not something that is a matter of indifference to Jesus Christ. We *can* learn to the glory of God, and we *ought* to learn to the glory of God. We *can* teach to the glory of God, and we *ought* to teach to the glory of God.

So, let us revisit how we know that 2+2=4 at all times and in all places.

Certainly we ourselves do not have universal knowledge of that fact. But we do all rely on the principle of induction (also called the uniformity of nature). No, we personally haven't experienced every instance of 2+2=4 in all places at all times. But, since every time we have experienced 2+2 in the past it has always equaled 4, we have good reason to believe that it will always work out that same way in the future.

If left just like that, how does that teaching glorify God?

The answer: it doesn't.

Unless we have a God who has revealed to us that we can rely on the uniformity of nature, we have no *logical* reason to base any universal truth claims on the principle of induction. Let us stay together on this . . . In the *past*, two plus two has always equaled four. But logically, that doesn't give us *any* indication that two plus two will equal four in the future. The only way we would know that is if (1) we already know the future, or (2) someone who does know the future has revealed it to us.

This is the case in Christianity. God *has* declared that because he is a God, not of chaos but of order (1 Cor 14:33), he has ordained the uniformity of nature as a foundation for us to build reliable patterns of thought (Gen 1:14, 8:22; cf. Ps 104:19; Luke 12:54–55). But it is only in trusting in him and his word—with genuine intentionality—that we are able to fully grasp not just facts about the world around us, but also the true philosophy of facts that underlie our interpretation of them. And it is then, from that foundation, that we are able to glorify God in knowing and applying 2+2=4. And this example of 2+2=4 is just a very basic and simple example, which now brings us to *Christian Education*.

Christian Education

Christian education *is* Christian discipleship.

We were born into sin (Ps 51:5); we were *re*born into the likeness of Christ (Eph 2:4–5, 4:20–24). Formerly our minds were futile (Eph 4:17) and our thinking was darkened (Eph 4:18). But now, God has "delivered us from the domain of darkness and transferred us to the kingdom of his beloved Son" (Col 1:13).

It is now from him, the true Light of the world (John 1:4–5, 9), that we are able to escape the darkened nature of our sinful minds and learn to bring *every thought* "captive to obey Christ" (2 Cor 10:5)!

Introduction: Christian Education

We ourselves are first and foremost disciples, not of uninterpreted facts, but disciples of Christ. He is not just King of our souls but King of all the universe (Ps 2:8–12; cf. Matt 28:18; Heb 1:3). This, in turn, means that if we are to teach on anything in the universe, and if we are to honor him in our teaching, we must teach any and every fact as it relates to the person and work of Jesus Christ. For indeed, not only is he the creator of all things (John 1:3; Col 1:16; Heb 1:2), but in him all things hold together and derive their true meaning (Col 1:17; Heb 1:3).

In short, we cannot learn or teach any subject as if that subject is possible whether or not Jesus Christ is Lord. It is on this principle we must be fully committed when it comes to Christian education. It is *only* because Jesus Christ is Lord and reigns supreme (Col 1:16–17; Phil 2:9–11), that we can have any true knowledge about any fact on any subject at all.

As it relates to our children, Christian education *is* the Great Commission (Matt 28:18–20), carried out in the most basic unit of the world-order that God has ordained: the family. And the goal of Christian education as it pertains to our children is to make fully mature disciples of Christ.

That is to say, the goal of Christian education is not simply to lead our children into trusting in Christ for their salvation (though in God's sovereign election and the power of the Holy Spirit that is part of it). Rather, the continuing goal of Christian education is to further our children along in their salvation by teaching them not to be futile and darkened in their thinking (Eph 4:17), but continually to be renewed in their minds (Eph 4:23) whereby they are better able to glorify God in all that they do (1 Cor 10:31), including all that they think and *how* they think.

The secular-humanist, state-sponsored schools cannot and will not educate this way.

This is why we homeschool.

So, with this definition in mind, let us read on and consider the meaning and significance of Christian education as well as the difference we will see when we consider whether our children should be taught by us at home or be taught by the secular-humanist, state-sponsored curriculum of our day.

Section 1

The Meaning of Christian Education
The Fear of the Lord is the Beginning of Knowledge

KNOWLEDGE IS NOT NEUTRAL.

We are surely familiar with the parable Jesus taught about the man who hears the word of the Lord and obeys it. Jesus says he is like a man who builds his house on the rock (Matt 7:24–27). In this parable, the storm comes for both parties. There is no escaping it in a fallen world. While the man who builds his house on sand (something other than Christ), watches his house come crumbling down, it is the man who builds his life on the Rock, which is Christ, who is able to withstand the storm.

So, the question becomes: Upon which surface do we want our children to build their house? On the sand of human wisdom (1 Cor 1:18–20, 2:14; Isa 2:22), or on the foundation of Jesus Christ (Col 1:16–17, 2:3)?

If we trace the idea of acquiring knowledge and wisdom (learning facts *and* a system of interpreting those facts) throughout the Scriptures, we'll soon find that it *begins and ends* with the Lord.

Solomon wrote that the fear of the Lord is "the *beginning* of knowledge" (Prov 1:7, emphasis mine). Then later he wrote that when all is said and done, the end or goal of knowledge (and all of experience) is the same thing: "Fear God and keep his commandments" (Eccl 12:13).

It's not as though we are told in Scripture to begin our thinking with some alleged neutral standard, and then after everything is considered, if God passes our test, then we can allow him into our thought process. Rather, the fear of God is to be at the very *beginning* of our thinking. *That* is the foundation to how we view and consider everything in the universe.

But it doesn't stop there.

Since the Lord Jesus Christ is not only the creator of all space-time facts (John 1:3; Col 1:16) but also the sustainer of all space-time facts (Col 1:17; Heb 1:3), then every fact we learn (whether it be a fact of literature, math, science, history, etc.) must be related to him and his lordship.

As such, these facts have a goal. No one is to learn anything just for the sake of knowledge (1 Cor 8:1–2). Rather, everything we do and learn is to be done and learned for the sake of glorifying God (Rom 11:36; 1 Cor 10:31; Col 3:17).

What is God's paradigm for learning in this way and teaching our children in this way? Or, asked another way, how do we lead our children in building their house on the Rock of Jesus Christ?

Chapter 1

Christ
The Foundation, Means, and Goal of All Knowledge

"In him are found all the treasures of wisdom and knowledge..."
—COLOSSIANS 2:3

THE LORDSHIP OF JESUS Christ is not an afterthought when it comes to how we learn any or every subject or fact. Rather, (this really bears repeating) as he is the creator and sustainer of all facts (Col 1:16–17), whenever we learn any fact on any subject, to learn it fully we must learn it in its relation to him.

It is the unbeliever, as a condition of and judgment on his sin, who is futile in his mind and thinking (Rom 1:21; Eph 4:17) and darkened in his heart and understanding (Rom 1:21; Eph 4:18). Before we were regenerated by the Holy Spirit we were the same way (Titus 3:3, 4–7). But now that we are believers (by his power—Eph 2:1–10), we are never commanded to take the mind of Christ off in order to learn "on a level playing field" with the unbeliever.

To the contrary, since we have the mind of Christ, we are to be continually renewed in our minds in him (Eph 4:23), to the point that we daily attempt (by his power working in us—Col 1:29) to take *every thought* captive to obey him and live under his lordship (2 Cor 10:5).

This means that when we learn any fact on any subject, we don't attempt to learn it as if it *could be* a fact whether or not Jesus is Lord. The only reason it is a fact at all, and that we can recognize it as such, is precisely *because* Jesus is Lord (Heb 1:3a). And to truly know it, we must learn it in that light (Ps 36:9).

Consequently, when we learn 2+2=4, we don't simply accept it as a universal truth for pragmatic reasons. We learn it in a way that is based on the lordship of Christ as the creator and sustainer of 2+2=4. It is no longer to us a universal truth in which we trust through blind faith simply because it makes it easy to get by in this world. Rather, trusting in this application of the principle of induction is a living and active faith in the very one who has revealed it to us from his word (Gen 1:14, 8:22; cf. Ps 104:19; Luke 12:54–55). Furthermore, contrary to learning it for pragmatic reasons as its end game, we learn it in order to glorify God whenever and however we come to apply 2+2=4 and the principles and applications involved in that knowledge.

In other words, all knowledge—all true knowledge—must have at its foundation a fearful trust in the Lord (Prov 1:7), must be acquired through the means he has provided (Col 1:16–17), and must have as its aim to glorify him (1 Cor 10:31). That's a tall order to be sure. What is the practical application? For our purposes here, we should examine the mere basic course categories in most state education programs (which we will do in section two). For now, let us examine a little bit more of this claim.

Christ: The Foundation of All Knowledge

How are we to begin our thinking? That might seem like an odd question, but it's an important one indeed. In the garden of Eden, man was given the opportunity to begin his thinking by relying on the revelation of God. This, Adam did for a while, as he obeyed God in naming the animals and exercising dominion over them

(Gen 2:19).[1] He was relying on God's revelation to him that that was indeed one of the tasks for which he was created.

But not too long after he and Eve were getting along quite well in paradise, the serpent approached Eve and convinced her not to rely on God's revelation—that eating the fruit would bring death—but to rely on her own ability in her thinking (to "be her own person" as is sometimes the catchphrase of our day). Instead of thinking *in submission* to God's revelation, the serpent wanted her to think *apart* from God's revelation (Gen 3:4–5).

That is what Scripture says regarding this encounter. Rather than relying on the knowledge that God had revealed to her about that particular fruit, which she fully knew (Gen 3:3), she instead decided to choose for herself how she would think about the tree:

> So when the woman saw that the tree was good for food, and that it was a delight to the eye, and that the tree was to be desired to make one wise, she took of its fruit and ate, and she also gave some to her husband who was with her, and he ate. (Gen 3:6)

Adam, who was with her, abandoned the first principle of applied knowledge (Prov 1:7), and instead of humbly relying on God's revelation, tried to decide for himself about whether or not that tree would "make one wise."

It turns out, the tree didn't make him wise, but, just as God promised, brought a curse of death upon him and all his posterity. Because of Adam's sin we are all now in the curse of death (Rom 5:12–14). And we all, without being regenerated by God, have a corrupt thought life in heart and mind (Eph 4:17–18).

Scripture says that true knowledge and true wisdom comes when, at the very outset, we begin all our endeavors of thought in

---

1. For an excellent resource on a profound case study showing the significance of Adam's naming the animals as an exhibition of his having dominion over them and partaking in the education process under God's authority, see chapter five of Stephen C. Perk's *The Christian Philosophy of Education Explained*. The other chapters are extremely helpful as well in understanding the topic of Christian education and its underlying philosophy.

the fear of the Lord (Prov 1:7, 9:10), relying on his revelation to guide us (Ps 36:9, 119:105).

Conversely, when we despise his instruction (Prov 1:7b), and suppress our natural inclination to begin our thinking with him while "claiming to be wise," we truly become fools (Rom 1:22), which produces even more futility in our thinking and foolishness in our hearts (Rom 1:21).

Christ is not merely the conclusion of our thinking. Rather, if he is to have his rightful place in our lives, he must also be the very foundation of our thinking. For it is in him—and in him alone—"in whom are hidden *all* the treasures of wisdom and knowledge" (Col 2:3, emphasis mine):

> For *from* him and through him and to him are all things. To him be glory forever. Amen. (Rom 11:36, emphasis mine)

But will our children learn to see Christ in his rightful place as the *foundation of all knowledge* from the secular-humanist, state-sponsored curriculum? We think the answer is obvious. However, we must not stop there. Christ is not only the foundation of all our knowledge, but he is the very means for how we acquire knowledge.

Christ: The Means of All Knowledge

Unbelievers *do* know things. This is because of what theologians typically call natural revelation and common grace. Now, theologically, those two things are distinguished. Natural revelation is the revelation God has given about himself in the nature of the created order. Paul gives reference to this in Romans 1:19–20:

> For what can be known about God is plain to them, because God has shown it to them. For his invisible attributes, namely, his eternal power and divine nature, have been clearly perceived, ever since the creation of the world, in the things that have been made.

See Psalm 19:1–6 for another expression of how God's created universe clearly points to him.

However, Paul goes on to say that because of man's sinful nature, even though he knows this about God, he suppresses that truth (Rom 1:18, 21–22).

And yet God is still gracious to man. He allows man to get along with his life in spite of his unwillingness to love and worship him (Matt 5:45; Acts 14:16–17). He allows unbelieving man—who does not base his knowledge on the fear of the Lord—to grow in peripheral knowledge about his world. He allows unbelieving man to have dominion over animals, to develop and use tools, to create and play instruments (Gen 4:20–22). He designed history so that all men—including unbelievers—will increase in knowledge through time, even as travel increases across the world (Dan 12:4). This is all due entirely to God's common grace.

Man was created in God's image (Gen 1:27). And even though sin has marred that image, we are still graciously given the capacity to think and learn and develop—even while not doing it from the foundation of his word or toward his glory (Gen 11:3–4).

> For from him and *through* him and to him are all things. To him be glory forever. Amen. (Rom 11:36, emphasis mine)

It is because of how God created us—as image bearers of himself—that we have the physical and cognitive faculties to learn, to be educated, and to teach others (Gen 1:26–28; cf. Ps 8:4–8). But if we send our children to be discipled by a secular-humanist, state-sponsored curriculum, will they be taught that it is *only because of the gracious work of God* that they are able to grow in knowledge (Prov 2:6)? Again, we think the answer is obvious.

Nonetheless, whether believer or unbeliever, we are able to acquire knowledge about God's world. It is here where the believer and unbeliever have commonality in education. The problem is that when knowledge is acquired from the wrong foundation or done to the glory of someone or something other than him, unless the recipients of that knowledge repent and relearn it in light of

Christ and for his glory (Eph 4:17–24), it ends up being all for naught (Matt 16:26).

For the foundation of our learning must be the word of our Lord (Matt 7:24–27; John 17:17). And the ends to which our learning is accomplished must be the glory of our Lord (Rom 11:36; 1 Cor 10:31; Col 3:17). Otherwise, the knowledge we gain from his world, even through the very means he has provided, is only "what is falsely called 'knowledge'" (1 Tim. 6:20–21) when it does not relate back to him.

So we ask again, will our children learn any of this if we send them to be discipled by a secular-humanist, state-sponsored curriculum? Further, we must also ask to what end should education be directed?

Christ: The Summation of All Knowledge

From our earlier discussion, we determined the glory of our Lord is the goal of all knowledge. The purpose of any and all knowledge is not to build ourselves up for our own sakes. Yes, we are to have dominion over the world he created (Gen 1:26–28; Ps 8:4–8); but that dominion is to be for his glory alone (Ps 115:1; Isa 42:8; Rev 4:9–10, 11).

It is because of him alone that we are able to live and move and have our being (Acts 17:28). Therefore, it is he alone in whom the glory of our efforts ought to have their ultimate end. As the apostle Paul said, "I worked harder than any of them, though it was not I, but the grace of God that is with me" (1 Cor 15:10), so we too must recognize that no matter what we accomplish in this life, it is only by the sovereign, gracious will of our Lord that we have any desire to do it, and it is through his own power that we're able to bring it about (Col 1:29). We are mere vessels in his hand. So, clearly he ought to receive the glory of all that we accomplish—and this certainly includes anything and everything that we accomplish in our life of knowledge, wisdom, and education.

CHRIST

> For from him and through him and *to* him are all things. *To him* be the glory forever. Amen. (Rom 11:31, emphasis mine)

This is for all things, but in Scripture there is a specific warrant for glorifying God in the realm of education (Prov 25:2; cf. Ps 115:1, 16, 18) as a part of the cultural mandate to have dominion (Ps 8:6–8). And we must teach this to our children as we disciple them in a Christian worldview.

So, with Christ as our foundation, means, and goal of all knowledge, our next question is: How is this knowledge and understanding to be gained by our children?

Chapter 2

Parents

The Stewards of Discipleship

"You shall teach them diligently to your children . . ."

—DEUTERONOMY 6:7

WHILE THERE ARE ACCOUNTS in Scripture of certain people of God receiving both private, nonparental education (Paul—Acts 22:3; cf. Gal 1:14) and state-sponsored education (Daniel—Dan 1:3–4, though in Daniel's case it was coerced slavery), the only *imperative* concerning education is directed toward parents themselves (Deut 6:1–7; Eph 6:4).

Context here is key. While we think the below passage, which will occupy our attention for the remainder of this chapter, is *applicable* to the modern concept of homeschooling, we would do well to look at the passage in its entirety to get a much clearer understanding of our marching orders and their original intent:

> Hear, O Israel: The LORD our God, the LORD is one. You shall love the LORD your God with all your heart and with all your soul and with all your might. And these words that I command you today shall be on your heart. You shall teach them diligently to your children and shall

talk of them when you sit in your house, and when you walk by the way, and when you lie down, and when you rise. (Deut 6:4–7)

Taken at surface value, this passage is not strictly speaking about educating our children in the *subjects* of literature, math, science, history, etc. It is first and foremost speaking of our obligation to disciple our children in *knowing the Lord*. This, of course, flies right in the face of our modern understanding of education.

Our culture tells us that what we really want to ensure is that our children spend six and a half hours a day, *five days a week* learning literature, math, science, history, etc. from a state-sponsored, secular-humanist curriculum, and only an hour or two (if that) *one day out of the week* learning about the Lord and his commands. But God tells us that what we really ought to be doing is teaching our children about God and his commands, not an hour a week, not six and a half hours a day throughout the weekdays, but *all throughout the day, each and every day*.

That is Christian education. That is Christian discipleship. And that is the purpose of homeschooling and raising our children.

It sounds a little odd, doesn't it? If all our children know is the Lord and his commands, how practical is that? The last time we checked, our children would most likely not be able to get a job by giving their testimony of the graciousness of Jesus and then reciting the Ten Commandments or the Sermon on the Mount.

Well, before we get into the full scope of what knowing the Lord and his commands truly entails, let us just briefly examine this question right here. If we're honest with ourselves, it seems evident that the most practical thing our children can do as they grow up is to know the Lord.

> And this is eternal life, that they *know* you the only true God, and Jesus Christ whom you have sent. (John 17:3, emphasis mine)

> Blessed is the man
> who walks not in the counsel of the wicked,
> nor stands in the way of sinners,

nor sits in the seat of scoffers;[1]
but his delight is in the *law of the* LORD,
and on his law he meditates day and night . . .
In *all* that he does, *he prospers* . . .
(Ps 1:1–2, 3, emphasis mine)

It is not the one who walks in the secular-humanist, state-sponsored curriculum who prospers in all that he does (even *if* he is somehow better at doing algebra or knows more about the periodic table of elements, etc.). Rather, Scripture tells us clearly that the one who truly prospers in all that he does is the one who meditates on the law of the Lord, not just six and half hours a day each weekday, but every day and all throughout the day ("day and night").

So, even if the children being taught mathematical, scientific, historical, or geographical facts by the state *were* to know more about those things than our children who are being discipled in knowing the Lord and his commands, it appears even then that our children are the ones who are being set up to succeed in life (*eternal* life no less) much better than their state-discipled counterparts.

However, just in case we are not convinced about this, let us remember that even if our children discipled in the Lord do not have more *worldly success* in this life, which certainly can be the case, regardless of how intelligent they are or how much they know (Ps 73), Jesus gives us a very good perspective regarding success in the world versus knowing him: "For what will it profit a man if he gains the whole world and forfeits his soul?" (Matt 16:26).

Our primary concern in Christian education—that is, Christian discipleship—is and always should be to lead those under our care in knowing the Lord and his commands. Sadly, many of us Christian parents for far too long have been hoodwinked into thinking our primary job as Christian parents is to see that our

---

1. If anything can be considered the counsel of the wicked, the way of sinners, the seat of scoffers, it is the secular-humanist, state-sponsored curriculum, which is the focal point of all state education.

children get a good education (regardless of its secular-humanist, state-sponsored foundation), so that they can be successful in life (meaning so that they can get a good job and live the American dream).

It hasn't at all dawned on us that in order for them to be most successful in life and be able to prosper in *all* that they do, we must ourselves obey the word of God in teaching our children about him and his commands all throughout the day, every day. Yet that is precisely what Scripture tells us (Deut 6:1–7; Ps 1:1–3).

Now having said that, believe it or not, what we shall discover in our unwrapping of this text is that knowing the Lord and his commands does not mean simply reading the Bible and that's all there is to it. To the contrary, his commands entail us to have dominion over the world and so be fluent in the various subjects of knowledge. Furthermore, because our children's education will be rooted in the word of God at every turn, we are confident that they will know more about what they study than they ever would have under the secular-humanist, state-sponsored education system.

And to see that, let us begin our closer examination of this passage.

The Lord is One

To a certain degree it makes sense to speak of *subjects* in order to have a rough framework around our knowledge categories of facts and their interpretation. And it actually makes it quite convenient. However, to compartmentalize *subjects* as the secular-humanist, state-sponsored curriculum does, is to deny the sovereign and unifying triune God who reigns over every fact and its interpretation and unites them all to himself. Let us explore this, just with one example (which we will revisit in section two): *language*.

Is language important? Of course it is. It's how we communicate. But why do we communicate this way? How did human language, as we know it (whether oral or written), become the medium for our communication? Was a system of language itself created at a point in the history of the human race as universal knowledge?

Or did it evolve over time from grunts or other sounds? Did different languages come into existence because of the Lord's intervention in history (whether natural or supernatural), or are their variations explained by some other reason? Does language reflect the creative and orderly mind of the triune God? Or is it merely an outworking of evolving organisms that eventually worked their way to mankind, as a pragmatic measure on their survival? What is the chief goal of language?

Just in answering the above questions, we can't merely speak of language, but are forced also to speak of history, of anthropology, of theology, of science, and on and on the list could go. All *subjects* (whether in Christian education or secular-humanist, state-sponsored curriculum) have a unifying nature behind them. And whether or not it is acknowledged, that unifying nature is the Lord Jesus Christ. As said before, he is the creator and sustainer of all facts and of all subjects (Col 1:16–17; Heb 1:3).

But we might be wondering, "What difference does this make when speaking of the separate *subjects* of literature, math, science, history, etc.?" The reality is, it makes all the difference in the world. The secular-humanist, state-sponsored curriculum would have our children believe there is an authority—an ultimate authority—for literature. But there is another ultimate authority for math. There is an ultimate authority for science. There is an ultimate authority for history, etc. All of these authorities are *ultimate* in their own domain; yet none of these authorities will go back to one *actual* ultimate authority that has the final say when any thought from one subject comes into conflict with a thought from another subject. Least of all will they go back to the one true ultimate authority—the Lord Jesus Christ (Matt 28:18; Col 1:16–17; Heb 1:3).

We recognize that this *may* seem trivial. So, let us look at one illustration in order to see how this plays out in a practical level:

What is truth? How is it determined?

With just those two questions, our children will not find a unifying answer in the various authorities from the secular-humanist, state-sponsored curriculum.

The Christian answer is that truth is reality as created, sustained, and interpreted by the triune God. But in secular-humanist, state-sponsored curriculum the answer(s) will be very different.

In the literature curriculum, our children will be told that truth is one's *own* perception of reality (or an author's perception of reality), determined by individual human minds. What is true for one person will not necessarily be true for another.

In the natural sciences curriculum, our children will be told that truth is what corresponds to reality—as interpreted by the authorities of academia. For instance, while macro evolution has not been demonstrated by repeatable observation, we know it is true because the authorities have said so. And when taken as true, it corresponds to reality as *they* interpret it.

In the social sciences curriculum, our children will be told that truth is unknowable, as the lasting account of it is generally written by the victors of history. So, while truth is unknowable, truth varies depending on who is winning or has won the wars (whether military wars or culture wars).

Think about what our children would have just learned about truth. It's determined by themselves, *and* it's determined by reality as interpreted by the authorities of academia. Yet at the same time truth is unknowable and has a subset of truth that changes depending on who controls the culture and has written the history books.

Yet the answer *we* as Christians can give our children, from a Christ-centered worldview, is so much simpler and is the only way we can truly interpret the world around us. The Lord Jesus Christ is himself truth incarnate (John 14:6), and only he has the rightful position to interpret himself, the world he created, and how the two correspond.

If we send our children to be taught from the secular-humanist, state-sponsored curriculum they will hear anything and everything *but* this idea of truth. Yet it is this very idea of truth that is supposed to set us and our children apart from the rest of the world (John 17:17).

In the secular-humanist, state-sponsored curriculum, competing ultimate authorities are at war with each other, and there is no final authority to unify knowledge in those subjects. There is a word for this. We may not like it, but it's the correct word to describe it: polytheism. No, we're not saying that all children in the government schools are polytheists. As a religion it is almost certain that only a fraction of a tiny percentage of them are (if even that—unless we count Mormonism). But in a practical sense, their education is in a polytheistic system. Each subject (or domain) has its own ultimate authority. And there is no true, final (actual *ultimate*) authority for all knowledge to unify what they learn in their education.

But what does Scripture say about that?

> For although there may be so-called gods in heaven or on earth—as indeed there are many "gods" and many "LORDS"—yet for us there is one God, the Father, from whom are all things and for whom we exist, and one Lord, Jesus Christ, through whom are all things and through whom we exist. (1 Cor 8:5–6)

Or, from the text we have before us, we need to recognize how God starts his command for us to teach our children. It begins with "the Lord is One" (Deut 6:4). In the context of the Ten Commandments, God had just rescued Israel from the polytheistic tyranny of Egypt. Using plagues that corresponded to the very gods of that society, he demonstrated that he alone had authority over all creation and that their gods had no authority over him.

The Lord indeed was and is the final and ultimate authority. Thus, the beginning of his call to Israel is: "Hear, O Israel: The Lord our God, the Lord is one" (Deut 6:4). And it is only by interpreting all of life through the foundation of him and his word that we can make sense out of the world he created.

The fact that he must be at the beginning of our thinking is the foundation to how we bring up our children in the discipline and instruction of the Lord (Eph 6:4); and it is only in that light that the various subjects we learn will truly be cohesive, as they all relate back to him. But, there is another key aspect to our obligation in raising our children as disciples of Christ.

You Shall Love the Lord Your God

It's not enough to believe in God without having a saving knowledge of him. As James says, "You believe that God is one; you do well. Even the demons believe—and shudder!" (Jas 2:19). Christian education (or as we have been rightly calling it, Christian discipleship) is not a paradigm of simply getting the correct formula, putting our children through the program, and *voila*: fully mature Christian disciples.

Christian education involves the whole of Christianity worked out in daily life. It's not as though our intention ought to be to teach our children about God and his commands day and night—merely for the sake of being *right* in our approach to education. But even at the beginning of that command we have our own personal, relational responsibility to the Lord—to love him ourselves.

> *You* shall love the LORD your God with all *your* heart and with all *your* soul and with all *your* might. And these words that I command you today shall be on *your* heart. (Deut 6:5–6, emphasis mine)

Our children will not merely be interested in *what* we teach them about God and his commands. But they will be just as interested in *how* we teach them about God and his commands—perhaps even more so. That is why James is so concerned with how many teachers ought to be in the church (Jas 3:1). He goes on in his illustration concerning the tongue (Jas 3:2–12) and then concludes: "Who is wise and understanding among you?" That is, "Who should be a teacher among you?"—"By his good conduct let him show his works in the meekness of wisdom" (Jas 3:13).

Being a good teacher involves the whole person having good conduct and works done in the meekness of Christian wisdom. And it is impossible to have and display that kind of demeanor apart from a loving, saving knowledge of the Lord Jesus Christ ourselves (1 John 4:19; Titus 3:3–7).

As a great example of this, it would do us well to look at the apostle Paul. He viewed the churches he planted as his children (1 Cor 4:14–16) and instructed them plainly: "Be imitators of me, *as I am of Christ*" (1 Cor 11:1, emphasis mine).

If we attempt to train our children in the ways of the Lord but do not ourselves have a love for our Savior and his commands, it will eventually become evident to our children (Matt 7:15–20). And while our gracious God can still save them and disciple them to a wonderful understanding of himself, the natural course of action, and his command to us as parents, is for us to love him ourselves, and demonstrate that love by obeying his commands (John 14:15).

Now, we have spoken much about God and his commands, all the while assuming a knowledge of the gospel. But we ought to make it clear that the gospel is at the very root of knowing the Lord and his commands:

> And this is eternal life, that they know you the only true God, and Jesus Christ whom you have sent. (John 17:3)

> Abide in me, and I in you. As the branch cannot bear fruit by itself, unless it abides in the vine, neither can you, unless you abide in me. (John 15:5)

> In this is love, not that we have loved God but that he loved us and sent his Son to be the propitiation for our sins. (1 John 4:10)

> We love because he first loved us. (1 John 4:19)

We cannot, no matter how hard we try, love God without first being transformed and regenerated by him (Titus 3:4–7). He is the one who gives us a new heart (Ezek 36:26–27; cf. 2 Cor 5:17). And even after being regenerated in a new birth, we cannot think we will be successful if we attempt to teach our children the Lord and his commands if we rely on our own fleshly strength to do it (Gal 3:3). Only by relying on him for our faith in the gospel *and* for our continued sustenance in spiritual strength will we be able to rightly teach our children about the Lord Jesus Christ and his commands.

> Finally, be strong *in the Lord* and in the strength of *his might*. (Eph 6:10, emphasis mine)

> *Him* we proclaim, warning everyone and teaching everyone with all wisdom, that we may present everyone mature in Christ. For this I toil, struggling with all *his* energy that *he* powerfully works within me. (Col 1:28, 29, emphasis mine)

There is no mask authentic-looking enough that we can wear when it comes to our relationship with the Lord Jesus Christ. We cannot act or fake a relationship with him (Matt 7:21–23; 2 Tim 2:19). And only by having a genuine, loving, saving, trusting relationship with him are we able to truly teach our children how to be his disciples.

So, if making our children disciples of Christ is the goal of Christian education, it starts with us first being his disciples. Or, as in the text before us, *we* are first to love the Lord our God with all *our* soul and with all *our* might (Deut 6:5). It is only by relying on his Spirit that we are able to do that (Rom 8:1–2, 5) and consequently have the words that he commands on *our* hearts (Deut 6:6). Then and only then are we able to continue in the rest of the passage.

You Shall Teach Them Diligently to Your Children

What we have learned about our responsibility so far as Christian parents is that everything we teach our children must relate to the final authoritative lordship of our triune God, which is summed up in Jesus Christ (Eph 1:9–10). We must teach them that all of knowledge and education begins with seeing him and him alone as the final authority to all areas of knowledge, by which they get their coherence. In that light, we have seen that the most important thing we teach our children is not the various state-sanctioned *subjects*, but rather that we teach them about God and his commands.

Furthermore, we have seen that we cannot fulfill our responsibilities as Christian parents if we do not first have a saving knowledge of the Lord Jesus Christ. It is only by him saving us and transforming us that we will then be able to teach our children about our God, his commands, and most importantly, his graciousness in declaring us righteous and progressively making us righteous through the death and resurrection of Christ and the work of the Spirit.

Though it may give us discomfort to go into this next part of the passage, it really cannot be any clearer:

> *You* shall teach them (that is, his commandments) diligently to *your* children, and shall talk of them when *you* sit in your house, and when *you* walk by the way, and when *you* lie down, and when *you* rise (Deut 6:8, emphasis mine).

In the context of this passage, there were no state-mandated, state-run, state-sponsored schools. There were no private schools either. So, what did the kids do all day? They learned about the Lord and his commands from *their own parents*. Whether at home, or walking to the market, or learning a trade, or waking up, or going to sleep—whatever they were doing—they were learning about the Lord and his commands. Or, at least their parents were charged with ensuring that is what was taking place.

So, it is here where we must repeat that the object of Christian education is to make Christian disciples. Not disciples of the state, nor disciples of the Renaissance, but disciples of Jesus Christ. Even apart from government schools, if we spend all our effort copying the secular-humanist, state-sponsored framework of education (and its various subjects) and just sprinkle in a nice little fact about the triune God throughout the curriculum, we have missed our obligation as Christian parents.

Our duty, day in and day out, is to instruct them about the Lord our God (who he is), his requirement for mankind (perfect righteousness), how we can meet that demand (trusting in Christ's righteousness on our behalf), and how we are to now live to his glory (in dependence on the Holy Spirit for a fruitful life of obedience).

These are the things we are to teach first and foremost to our children, and teach them *diligently*. But how is that worked out on a practical level? Surely even the children of Israel knew and sought more than merely a knowledge of the nature of God and our relationship to him, didn't they? Did they not also develop in their knowledge of the world and its relationship to God? Did they not also grow in how they understood literature, math, science, history, etc.?

Indeed, they did. And that brings us to what teaching God's commands truly entails.

Chapter 3

Children
The Foremost Disciples of the Great Commission

"Bring them up in the discipline and instruction of the Lord..."

—EPHESIANS 6:4

WHEN PAUL WROTE TO the audience of the letter of Ephesians, we must know that he had in the back of his mind Deuteronomy 6:4–7. He had just quoted the fifth of the Ten Commandments to them about the children's obligation to obey their parents (Eph 6:1–3; cf. Deut 5:16). And then he turns his attention to the parents, namely the fathers (to which we would do well to pay attention),[1] and says to them, "Fathers, do not provoke your children to anger, but bring them up in the discipline and instruction of the Lord" (Eph 6:4).

While there are myriad ways parents can provoke their children to anger, this work does not allow for an in-depth discussion

---

1. Even when speaking with homeschooling families, there are some fathers who think of the mother as the primary educator of the family. But when we look at this passage in Scripture along with the book of Proverbs as a whole "My son..." (from the father), it just doesn't seem to be the case. Both parents have a responsibility, certainly. But the father is the one ultimately responsible for his children's education.

of all of those things. Regarding education specifically, one way *not* to provoke them is for us parents to recognize that God has wired each of our children differently (see Gen 4:2b, 20–22a, 25:27). While math may come easily to one child, it may be very difficult for another. While one child may excel at oration, another may have great difficulty with it. What we must remember is that our children are not to be disciples of the Renaissance; they do not need training throughout their childhood to be polymaths. Rather they are disciples of the Lord Jesus Christ, and they need training throughout their childhood to use *whatever* natural abilities he has given them to take dominion over the earth for his glory, and use *whatever* spiritual gifts the Spirit gives them (1 Cor 12:4–11) for the glory of Christ and for the service of his church (Eph 4:7–16).[2]

Nevertheless, the latter part of the passage remains. We parents (and fathers specifically) have a true obligation to bring our children up in the discipline and instruction of the Lord. As we saw in the previous chapter, that means teaching them who God is and what he commands, and that our task is to do that every day, all throughout the day. The next question, then, is what all does that entail? What does it mean to teach them who God is and what he commands?

Here is our answer.

This is Eternal Life, that They Know You the Only True God

Without attempting to sound too repetitive, our priority in teaching them who God is must be centered in the gospel. The verse in its entirety is: "And this is eternal life, that they know you the only true God, and Jesus Christ whom you have sent" (John 17:3).

How does one know God? To teach them about God is to teach them about *all* of God (as he has revealed himself—Deut

---

[2]. This is not an argument against the classical Christian method of educating. I am actually drawn to that approach regarding method in pedagogy. I do not think this understanding of application is against that method. Regardless, the scope of this work is not to deal with method, but rather content.

29:29; John 1:17–18). As this present work is not a systematic or biblical theology, we will not go into detail here. However, to know who God is to know, as far as we can, all that Scripture has revealed to us about him, meaning we need to know for ourselves and teach to our children the God of Scripture as revealed in both Old and New Testaments.

Contrary to what is sometimes (or perhaps often) understood, these two sections of Scripture do not reveal opposing (or even complementary) gods. The God of the Old Testament is the *very same* God of the New Testament. In both portions of Scripture he is revealed as:

- Sovereign (Dan 4:35; cf. Rom 9:11–24)
- Holy (Isa 6:3; cf. Rev 4:8)
- Just (Deut 32:4; cf. Luke 18:1–8; Heb 2:2–3; Rev 16:7)
- Gracious, loving, and merciful (Exod 34:6–7 cf. Luke 10:21; 1 John 4:8; Luke 6:36)
- Transcendent (2 Chr 6:18; Isa 57:15a, 66:1; cf. Acts 7:48–50, 17:24–25)
- Immanent (Isa 57:15b; Ps 34:18; cf. John 1:14; Matt 28:20b)

Furthermore, both Old and New Testaments reveal him as having ultimate victory over the non-elect who are ever rebelling against him (Deut 32:39–42; Rev 11:17–18), and yet working mightily, in unity with the three persons in himself, to redeem those whom he loves (Exod 14:13–14; Jer 31:33–34; cf. Rom 8:28–30; Heb 9:23–28; Rev 5:9–10).

This is who God is, and this is who we need to communicate to our children that he is, according to his word.[3] In order for our children to understand any of this, they need to be regenerated (1 Cor 2:14). However, regardless of their relationship to the Lord,

---

3. We won't belabor the point here, but sadly there is an entire generation of Christians who know very little of the Old Testament, when that is the very Scripture our Lord used in teaching theology, apologetics, ethics, and God's plan of redemption. We need to know both Old and New Testaments. And we need to teach both Old and New Testaments to our children.

our obligation as parents (Deut 6:7) and teachers of truth (John 14:6, 17:17; 3 John 4) is to teach them the God of the Bible and what he commands. Yet, is Scripture the only place where we are to learn about our Lord?

Teaching Them to Observe All that I have Commanded You

And now we come to that final, practical piece for those who are worried that if we follow this book thus far, our children will have no functional means of providing for themselves as adults.

Here, our good friends, we pray it starts to come together.

The Great Commission is a redeeming of the cultural mandate. Whatever Jesus did in teaching new commandments, we must observe that he not once dismissed the teachings of the Old Testament. He upheld the law of the Old Testament at every turn (Matt 5:17–19, 23:2–3), confirming that the Scripture cannot be broken (John 10:35). While certainly the ceremonial aspect of the law has been completely fulfilled in his life, death, and resurrection (Heb 9:11–12), the moral law is still binding (Rom 7:12, 8:1–11, 13:8–10; cf. Gal 5:14). This moral law includes the command given to Adam and Eve at the very beginning: "Be fruitful and multiply and fill the earth and subdue it, and have dominion..." (Gen 1:26).

When God created Adam and Eve, he created them in his own image to be as sub-rulers under him over the entire earth. They were commanded to be fruitful (work productively), to multiply (procreate), to fill the earth (spread over the whole of creation—reflecting his glory over all the world), to subdue it (take charge over every nook and cranny), and have dominion (to master it; to rule over his creation as stewards). Having this mindset of God's creation and subduing it under his authority is another way to learn more about our Lord.

Sin, of course, ruined our desire and ability to carry out that mandate. Even after the global flood we see man trying to make a name for *himself* rather than acting as a sub-ruler *under* God and for *his* glory. The Tower of Babel illustrates this especially well

(Gen 11:1–9). Man was not being fruitful, but he was building a tower for his own glory. He was not filling the whole earth, but was staying in one location in order to carry out his own evil plans.

Then what happens? God intervenes. He confuses their language and disperses them over all the earth (Gen 11:9). And even now, though man is spread over all the earth, in his sinful state man is still trying to come together as one people and build a name for the glory of man.[4]

But then we turn to what is known as *the Great Commission*. Here the disciples are commanded to make disciples of *all* nations, teaching them everything Christ has commanded. As the Great Commission unfolds, rather than language being confused, it is being redeemed in that people are hearing the gospel in their very own language without hindrance (Acts 2:8).

Man is once again commissioned to reach the uttermost parts of the earth for the glory of God (the original mandate to fill the earth), but this time with his message of redemption (Acts 1:8). In other words, the cultural mandate has been redeemed and reclaimed.

It was part of our moral obligation to God all along, but with the good news of Jesus Christ comes the power to accomplish it (Acts 1:8). Instead of man living for himself and his own glory, trying to come together in the spirit of humanity, he can now, by the power of the Spirit of Jesus Christ, live for the glory of God, spreading out into the world with his message of redemption.[5]

And with that message of redemption also comes acts of redemption. Man can now truly have dominion over the earth in the power of the Spirit and for the glory of God.

---

4. The United Nations is a prime modern example of this sinful rebellion. While their intentions are seemingly good, the entire premise of their existence is that they, *as united nations*, can bring about world peace *without* the Lord Jesus Christ. See http://www.un.org/en/sections/un-charter/preamble/indExodhtml for more details.

5. For a better, clearer, and more thorough look at the relationship between the cultural mandate and the Great Commission, I recommend John Frame's book, *Salvation Belongs to the Lord*.

CHILDREN

How do we make entire nations disciples of the Lord Jesus Christ? It is not only through evangelism, though it is through that to be sure. But it is also through obeying the cultural mandate: being fruitful and multiplying and filling the earth and subduing it, and having dominion—and raising our children to do the very same thing.

It might be easier to see how great the Great Commission and the cultural mandate work together if we look at it this way:

- Be fruitful and multiply / Make disciples
- And fill the earth / of all nations
- And subdue it and have dominion / teaching them to observe all that I have commanded you.

These commands are not in contrast to one another; rather the Great Commission is a redemption and fulfillment of the cultural mandate. We are to be productive in our work (be fruitful), but adding to that, we are to teach others to be productive through Christ (make disciples). We are to procreate and spread throughout the whole of creation, reflecting his glory over all the world (multiply and fill the earth), but adding to that, we are to bring entire nations under the influence and lordship of Christ (*going* and *teaching* in order to make disciples of *all nations*). We are to rule over his creation as stewards (subdue the earth and have dominion over it), but adding to that, we are to make fully mature disciples who bring every thought captive to the lordship of Christ (teaching them to observe all that Christ has commanded).

Because the Lord Jesus Christ has all authority in heaven *and* on earth (Matt 28:18) and has promised to be with us (Matt 28:20b), we can be confident that the nations *will* be made his disciples (Matt 28:19–20a; cf. Ps 2:8, Dan 7:14, 27). But how is that done?

To be sure, the Great Commission adds responsibility to the cultural mandate. But it does not supplant it. And to be even more dogmatic, it should be clear that the Great Commission starts at home. The foremost disciples of the Great Commission and the cultural mandate should be our very own children.

In our very own home we need to be reclaiming the cultural mandate through the enabling power of the Spirit. We ourselves need to be taking dominion over the earth for the glory of God, and we need to be teaching our children to do the same.

Now, does all this mean we and our children must be masters of *every* part of knowledge in *every* field of knowledge? It is here where we would say no.

Because of the vastness of God's creation and the diversity of mankind, man needs others who can and will specialize in a field not their own. We need plumbers *and* physicians. We need engineers *and* mechanics. We need scientists *and* artists. None of us can be all of these things. We simply don't have that time (Ps 90:12).[6] But we do need to take dominion over the areas in which God has given us ability.

Despite how our culture has influenced our interpretation of Scripture, when Paul wrote, "I can do all things through him who strengthens me," (Phil 4:13), he was not at all indicating that the aim of Christian living was to be a Renaissance man.[7] Yes, we are supposed to have dominion over all the earth, but there is a limit to each one's knowledge (Eccl 8:16–17). Even in the early part of history, we see that God had so arranged for man to have specialization in his knowledge (Gen 4:20–22). And this is even magnified within the church as Paul speaks specifically of the various gifts of the body of Christ (Rom 12:3–8; 1 Cor 12:14–19).

We are to have dominion—to the glory of God—over every area in which we are able. But not every area in God's world will fall within our own domain. It is here again where our view of education will be at complete odds with the culture of state-governed curriculum, which expects every child to be the same in learning

---

6. Of course, if someone does have the time to learn all these things and, if learned, will use that knowledge to God's glory and for the love of his neighbor, terrific! Grace and peace be with you!

7. For those interested in knowing, the context seems clear enough that he was saying *through Christ* he has the ability to endure being poor and the ability to remain humble in having plenty.

ability, treats every child as if he or she is the same in learning capacity, demands that every child have the same results in every field, and also still promises that every child can be whatever he or she wants to be in this life.

It simply isn't so. Math is a good skill to know, but not all children will excel at math. Science is a terrific field to master, but not every child will have that capability. History is a wonderful counselor, but not every child will have the aptitude to learn from her to the same extent others will.

Our duty as parents is not to provoke our children to anger by insisting they master every part of knowledge there is. Scripture has plainly told us, it *cannot* be done:

> When I applied my heart to know wisdom . . . I saw all the work of God, that man cannot find out the work that is done under the sun. However much man may toil in seeking, he will not find it out. Even though a wise man claims to know, he cannot find it out. (Eccl 8:16–18)

Make no mistake. We will encourage and instruct our children to pursue knowledge (Prov 8:1–9:12); and our heart's desire and goal will be to provide an atmosphere where that kind of pursuit is most congenial. However, if our children are struggling with algebra, it is not for us to bring about a sense of guilt and shame until it finally clicks. Rather, our duty is to encourage our children (even through discipline; for our children shall not be lazy)[8] to use the abilities and gifts God *has* given them for his glory.

The tendency here is to worry that if they don't have dominion themselves over *all* areas of knowledge (if they're not Renaissance men and women—or even the modern state-sanctioned form of that type), then they won't get into a good college. But again, we must remind ourselves that our duty as parents is not to raise children so that they will get into a good college, but rather that they will be able to glorify God in whatever task to which

---

8. See Proverbs 6:6–11, 10:26, 13:4, 15:19, 19:24, 20:4, 21:25, 24:30–34, 26:14–16.

he calls them. College is merely an assumption on the part of our culture; but it is nowhere commanded in Scripture.[9]

Again, shall we encourage our children to seek after knowledge? Absolutely! Proverbs 8 (among many other passages) teaches the glory of seeking after wisdom and knowledge. It must be clear that if we neglect to teach a desire and thirst for knowledge, we are neglecting part of our parental responsibility. Our desire for them and how we bring them up in the discipline and instruction of the Lord should be that they would love to grow in knowledge daily—especially in the knowledge of our Lord and Savior Jesus Christ (John 17:3, 17:17; 2 Pet 3:18).

However, that does not mean they need to pursue being a Renaissance polymath. It means they need to seek the knowledge over the domain God has given them in their natural abilities. A broad base of knowledge is surely beneficial (which we will examine, in part, in the following section). But there will be a point at each child's life where specialization will need to start to occur.

Will they succeed if they go no further in math than the basics of arithmetic, but learn how to code beyond their peers? Will they succeed if they don't get a college degree but rather master their craft of oration, art, science, or whatever ability God has given them?

Scripture says they will:

> Do you see a man skillful in his work?
> he will stand before kings;
> he will not stand before obscure men.
> (Prov 22:29)[10]

---

9. Will we dissuade our children from attending college? It really depends on what their goal for attaining a college degree is. While sifting through that subject would probably require a whole book, in the meantime I highly recommend the chapter "Let the Christian Family Make Wise Choices for College," by Paul Michael Raymond and Aaron Hebbard in the book *95 Theses for a New Reformation*, ed. Aaron B. Hebbard.

10. In case one might be prepared to dismiss the above Proverb as simply not truly applicable to our age, we would recommend just looking at some facts and trends. For instance, in John Taylor Gotto's *Weapons of Mass Instruction*, he details the lives of world changers—past and present—who dropped out of

Instead of blindly following the culture of "get a college degree,"[11] we would rather teach them to work hard and be good at what they do—to the glory of God (Rom 11:36).

We are to train our children first and foremost to be disciples of the Lord Jesus Christ, using the talents and gifts he has given them through his power and for his glory. Part of that instruction is to train them to seek after knowledge and wisdom (Prov 8:10–11, 23:23). But part of that is to train them to realize their own limitations (Eccl 8:16–17) and be fruitful with *whatever* God has given them (Rom 12:3–8; 1 Pet 4:10–11). Regardless of what they learn, our hope is that it has been clear throughout, that whatever they learn, they learn it from the foundation of the lordship of Christ, that they learn it through recognizing the means he has given them to learn it, and that they learn it and apply it to his glory alone! For no matter what the secular-humanist world will try to say regarding man's abilities, the Christian must maintain at all times, what Paul recognized so long ago:

> For from him and through him and to him are all things. To him be glory forever. Amen. (Rom 11:36)

---

formal education, ranging from primary school to post-secondary school, to pursue informal education that allowed them to change not only their lives but the course of history. Furthermore, while certainly there are still many companies out there that, for whatever reason, require a bachelor's degree, many more companies are starting not to require one. Rather they simply look at the candidate's actual credentials. One prominent example is Google. See Ferenstein, "Why Google Doesn't Care about College Degrees, in 5 Quotes." Add to that the increasing number of modern individuals who are successful without having ever graduated college (See, for example, Smale "8 Hugely Successful People," and, Hudson, "100 Top Entrepreneurs Who Succeeded"), and the facts start to speak for themselves. But if you still are not convinced, my recommendation is to read about the college bubble in Charles Sykes's *Fail U.: The False Promise of Higher Education.* College will still be around tomorrow, but that doesn't mean it will still be needed to get a professional job.

11. Which at this point generally requires massive amounts of debt (see Prov 22:7).

Section 2

The Significance of Christian Education
Whoever is Not with Me is Against Me

KNOWLEDGE IS NOT NEUTRAL.

Our Lord—even in the flesh as he walked among us—said without qualification that whoever is not with him is against him (Matt 12:30).

In Christian education we have a paradigm of learning that is *with* Christ.[1] We recognize that the very beginning of knowledge is a fearful respect and awe of him and his lordship (Prov 1:7). We recognize that all that we know and learn must be related back to him as the creator and sustainer of all facts (Col 1:16–17, 2:3; Heb 1:3). And we, by the power of his Spirit in us, recognize that all that we learn must be learned and applied to his glory (1 Cor 10:31). From beginning to end, the Lord Jesus Christ is recognized as the sole owner, lender, and rightful benefactor of all that we learn and do (Rom 11:36).

This is not so with the secular-humanist, state-sponsored curriculum.

---

1. Not by our own intellect or will (1 Cor 1:28–31), but by the graciousness of him alone are we with him (Titus 3:4–7).

Since it is not, if we are to be biblically accurate, it is not enough to say that the secular-humanist, state-sponsored curriculum is neutral in regard to Christ. Rather, since it is not *with* him, it is truly *against* him and his lordship.

Because the secular-humanist, state-sponsored education system refuses to begin its curriculum with the fear of the Lord, refuses to acknowledge that anything we learn is by his hand, and refuses to give him glory for all that is learned, then we must, by necessity, be convinced that that education—that that discipleship—is not Christian.

Furthermore, if we are convinced that the primary responsibility of parents is to educate (that is, to disciple) our children to become disciples of Jesus Christ, then we must, of necessity, see that having the secular-humanist, state-sponsored curriculum be our children's primary discipler[2] is not simply a matter of being neutral toward raising our children to being disciples of Jesus Christ. Rather, it is, by nature of the case, actively raising them *not* to be disciples of the Lord Jesus Christ.

At worst the secular-humanist, state-sponsored curriculum outright denies the lordship of Christ, and at best, it treats his lordship with such relativity (that is, 2+2=4 regardless of whether Jesus Christ is Lord) that it borders on blasphemy.

The Lord, in his word, does not teach us to think this way; and to do so is to take the mind of Christ off—something which we are never commanded to do in Scripture. What is more—to teach others, especially children, to think this way is an abomination

---

2. Some Christian parents might object here and say that they can/do send their children to public schools and yet that they themselves are still their children's primary disciplers. One need only look at the math on this one. If our children are spending 6–8 hours a day, 5 days a week with a secular-humanist, state-sponsored discipler, teaching them a secular-humanist, state-sponsored worldview (or philosophy of facts), and only 2–3 hours with us, it becomes pretty clear who the discipler in our children's lives are. For more on this, I recommend watching the video series *Children of Caesar* by Voddie Baucham (produced by *American Vision*), and/or reading the book, *Already Gone: Why Your Kids Will Quit Church and What You can Do to Stop it*, by Ken Ham and Brit Beemer.

(see Luke 17:1–2; Matt 18:6). Meanwhile, Scripture is clear that a disciple (that is, student) *will become* like his teacher (Luke 6:40).

Some see their children as missionaries. But we must always remember that, according to Scripture, children are not yet ready for missionary work. They are, *by nature*, "tossed to and fro by the waves and carried about by every wind of doctrine" (Eph 4:14). The secular-humanist, state-sponsored schools are not missionary grounds for our children. They are seedbeds for temptation (temptation to reject or ignore the lordship of Christ either in deed or thought). And we know what our Lord says about sending our children into temptation:

> Temptations are sure to come, but woe to the one through whom they come! It would be better for him if a millstone were hung around his neck and he were cast into the sea than that he should cause one of these little ones to sin (Luke 17:1, 2; cf. Matt 18:6).

So, we must consider how great of a sin is it, if our responsibility is to disciple them from sunrise to sunset in knowing the Lord and his commands, but instead we send them to be discipled by a curriculum that constantly tempts them to ignore and reject the lordship of Christ at every turn?

Why do we homeschool our children?

Let us compare Christian education (Christian discipleship), which teaches that every thought must be captive to the obedience of Christ (2 Cor 10:5), to the secular-humanist, state-sponsored curriculum, which teaches that the lordship of Jesus Christ is irrelevant to the facts we learn and how we learn them. Then let us see if our children will be better equipped to be disciples of the Lord Jesus Christ—our main calling in life when it comes to our children—if we send them to be discipled by the secular-humanist, state-sponsored curriculum, or if we rather disciple them ourselves at home.

Chapter 4

Language Arts

In the secular-humanist, state-sponsored curriculum, what is the foundation and goal of the language arts? Even at the foundation of our thinking, what would the secular-humanist, state-sponsored curriculum teach our children about language? Let us review those questions asked earlier:

- How did human language, as we know it (whether oral or written), become the medium for our communication?
- Was a system of language itself created at a point in the history of the human race as universal knowledge? Or did it evolve over time from grunts or other sounds?
- Did different languages come into existence because of the Lord's intervention in history (whether natural or supernatural), or are their variations explained by some other reason?
- Does language reflect the creative and orderly mind of the triune God? Or is it merely an outworking of evolving organisms that eventually worked their way to mankind, as a pragmatic measure of their survival?
- What is the chief goal of language?

    We already know the answers to these questions.

From the secular-humanist, state-sponsored curriculum, our children will be taught that human language developed over time from grunts and sounds to what we have now. This happened through the process of macro-(and micro-) evolution as pre-man form became better and better over time, and eventually developed into man. Since various grunts and sounds over various parts of the earth developed at different times and in different places, we have diversity of language. The purpose of language is simply to communicate with other people and in the end is simply pragmatic. Though multiple languages are a barrier to communication, we have the capacity to unite in one language and we should look forward to the day we can do so.[1]

However, our Christian worldview has a very different foundation:

Human language was created by God as a means of communicating with *him* and our fellow man. It was present at the very beginning of man's history in the garden of Eden (Gen 2:16–17, 23), as a universal knowledge (see Gen 11:1). Being his own creation, it reflects the creativity and orderly mind of our Lord.

Different languages came into existence both supernaturally and naturally. God supernaturally created different languages as a judgment upon the rebellious people at the Tower of Babel (Gen 11:7). In addition to that, languages continued to experience variation naturally through God's spreading people out in order to keep them from coming back to their earlier model of using their own ingenuity in trying to become God (see Gen 11:8).

The chief goal of language, of course, is to glorify God by communicating with him and with others about him (1 Pet 2:9). We look forward to the day when the *judgment* of other languages is fully *redeemed* into a harmonious sound of all the languages singing his praises with one voice:

---

1. This truly is man's goal in the secular-humanist mindset. Even now the language "Esperanto" (introduced in 1887) is being learned throughout the world as "a second language for everyone." Even now, apart from the saving grace of our Lord, mankind is ever trying to get back to the Tower of Babel to unite together against him.

> After this I looked, and behold, a great multitude that no one could number, from every nation, from all tribes and peoples and languages, standing before the throne and before the Lamb, clothed in white robes with palm branches in their hands, and crying out with a loud voice, "Salvation belongs to our God who sits on the throne, and to the Lamb!" (Rev 7:9–10)

This is just the foundation to our language arts education (discipleship), and is there not such a vast difference when our Lord Jesus Christ is missing? Yet we must ask more questions to see how truly expansive the difference is:

- Whether it is reading, comprehending, evaluating, and/or appreciating literature, why is it taught in a secular-humanist, state-sponsored curriculum, and to what end?
- Why is writing as a discipline taught in a secular-humanist, state-sponsored curriculum, and to what end?
- Furthermore, what is the purpose of even having a foreign language requirement?

Of course, pragmatically, from the secular-humanist, state-sponsored curriculum it only makes sense to teach the rules of language so that our children can better communicate with the teacher and each other. But from a biblical standpoint, that cannot be the *only* foundation for learning language. As we have already seen, there was a time when people could communicate very well with everyone else, and they did it all in rebellion against the Lord and his commands (Gen 11:1–4).

Language is a useful tool without which we truly wouldn't be able to communicate with one another. But as we will see with all these subjects, pragmatism is the ethics behind the secular-humanist, state-sponsored curriculum. And pragmatism bases no foundation of knowledge on the fear of the Lord and gives no glory to the Lord in what is learned, how it is learned, or why it is learned. Sadly, there is nothing in language arts ethics that departs from this overarching theme in regard to the ethics of the secular-humanist, state-sponsored curriculum.

In the state-sponsored schools, our children would be told to learn to read and write in order to communicate better with other people. The reason for this usually ends up so that either (a) they can get into a good college, and/or (b) so that they can get a good job.

We could write extensively on the error of these points alone (even from the secular-humanist point of view), but the purpose of this section is to compare these types of foundations and ends of education with the Bible.

What about communicating with God? Is that at all important? From Scripture we know that even though he knows our thoughts before we speak them (Ps 139:1–4), we still have an obligation in Scripture to make our words as clear to him as we can (Ps 19:14; Eccl 5:1–2). Furthermore, words are not to be used simply in service to ourselves so that we might be able to get ahead of the other guy who doesn't have a good education or doesn't have a good job. Nor should they be taught as tools for such things. Our words are supposed to be used in *serving* others (Gal 5:13–15). When we write, it ought to be to serve the reader (Gal 6:11; 1 John 2:1).

Yet this teaching would be blatantly absent from any secular-humanist, state-sponsored curriculum. God is the founder of language (John 1:1), its perfect participant in it (Isa 55:11), and the primary recipient of it (Rev 7:9–10). He has also given us language as a tool in serving others for his glory. But in the secular-humanist, state-sponsored curriculum, he would not be mentioned at all to our children as language's founder, participant, or recipient. And language itself would be taught to our children primarily not as a tool to serve others but to serve themselves.

That alone is sufficient, we believe, for us not to send our children to be disciples of the secular-humanist, state-sponsored curriculum. But there is more at stake. For there is another side to writing; and that is reading. Why, in a secular-humanist, state-sponsored curriculum will reading be taught? And how would it be taught to our children? Further, how will our children be taught to evaluate what has been written? As usual, the pragmatic ethic is the answer. If our children can read, they can better get along in this life. They can pick out the right groceries; they can read books and magazines (and advertisements); they can travel better, etc.

And this is all true for the Christian as well. However, the purpose of knowing how to read for the Christian is first and foremost to be able to read the very word of God (Josh 1:8; Ps 1:2, 119:97–99; cf. Neh 8:8). To know him is eternal life (John 17:3) and to live for him is to be set apart from the world by his very own word (John 17:17). Obviously reading is an essential part of education and being able to live as a God-honoring, image-bearing creature, having dominion over the earth in his service for his glory. Reading certainly enhances that ability.

Can people honor him and live for his glory without knowing how to read? Absolutely. But as we are instructed to seek after knowledge (Prov 8), reading is probably the best skill we can learn. Because once we learn that, we can learn anything else (for which he has given us ability) that has been written down.

But there is another aspect to reading, which is discernment. How would our children be taught to evaluate, critique, and/or appreciate what others have written? From the secular-humanist, state-sponsored curriculum, this is one of the most pathetic areas. There is no unified, cogent standard on how to evaluate, critique, and/or appreciate literature. It ends up being *all* subjective.

To be clear, we can agree that there are elements to literature that God, in his good purposes, has made to be somewhat subjective. He has made some elements of literature more enjoyable to certain people, while other elements are more enjoyable to others. In that regard, there is a *sense* of subjectivity in literature.[2] And that's one of the many wonderful things about his word. It contains so many different styles of literature: narrative, law, history, poetry, songs, proverbs, letters, etc.

However, even in these various areas, none are subjective regarding their evaluation, critique, and appreciation. As a matter

---

2. We must consider that that very well may be part of the reason there is such diversity in his word. While we should be familiar with and study all of his word, there are certainly various parts of it which will be more attractive to us from a literary standpoint depending on how he created us.

of fact, we and our children are to think of God's word in whatever area it is expressed as the very standard of literature. In other words, when we evaluate poetry, we ought to compare it to the poetry of Scripture. When we evaluate history, we ought to compare it to the history of Scripture. When we evaluate songs or proverbs or prose, we ought to evaluate those things by comparing them to Scripture. And it is this evaluation standard that ought to be taught to our children.

Scripture is the very standard of literature; and our job as Christian parents is to teach that to our children.

But our children will not get this teaching from the secular-humanist, state-sponsored curriculum. To the contrary, the teaching they would receive from that curriculum is to evaluate *the Scriptures* based on the presuppositions of the modern or post-modern standard of literature. And of course, when that is done, the Scriptures fail the literature test. They fail because they claim absolute truth from the Christian God. While the modern standard of literature cannot tolerate the aspect of truth coming from the Christian God, the post-modern standard of literature cannot tolerate absolute truth of any kind.

Is it clear yet, just how against Christ (not *neutral* in regard to him, but *against* him) the secular-humanist, state-sponsored curriculum is? It will not present him and his word as the standard by which to evaluate all other literature. Rather, it presents him and his word as the test subject to be evaluated in light of all other literature. This teaching (that is, discipleship) is completely backwards according to how we are called as Christians, and how we as Christian parents are called to train our children (Luke 6:40; cf. John 17:17).

Lastly, we must briefly look at the foreign language requirement in the secular-humanist, state-sponsored schools. In brief, they mandate it only so that our children will have a "well-rounded" education (whatever that means). But it really doesn't mean a whole lot. How many of our secular-humanist, state-sponsored curriculum graduates are able to speak and interpret a foreign language? And even if they are, what purpose was given them to be able to do that other than being more marketable for a good college or good job, or simply being confident in their ability to travel to a foreign country and speak there comfortably as well?

In contrast, the Christian worldview teaches that if we are to learn a second (or third, or fourth) language, it too is to be in the service of God and for his glory. It's a reversal of the curse and the judgment upon mankind when God confused the languages. A foreign language (or foreign languages) is (or are) to be learned in order to better speak to other people about the graciousness of God,[3] proclaiming the excellencies of him who called us out of darkness into his marvelous light (1 Pet 2:9) to people in their own language, as well as to further the cultural mandate in other areas of the world.

While this was done miraculously at Pentecost (Acts 2:6–11), God even now uses this natural ability with those gifted in learning multiple languages to accomplish his will throughout the earth. This, our friends, is the purpose of learning a foreign language. And it is for this purpose that we will teach foreign languages to our children (as far as God gives them ability).

To that end, certainly not everyone is gifted in that area, and so for them it should not be required. However, some are even gifted in learning languages that are no longer spoken. For years this has brought the church great insights into the wonderful word of God and the revelation of that word to us, his children.

Language was created by God for us to communicate with him and each other. Learning it with God as the foundation and with his glory as the focal point is the only biblical option for the Christian and our children. Learning it from a secular-humanist, state-sponsored, allegedly *neutral* foundation (that is in actuality *against* the lordship of Christ)—and that only for pragmatic purposes—is not Christian discipleship. Therefore, we cannot maintain both that our role as parents is to train our children to

---

3. This of course does not preclude learning "dead" languages so as to have a better grasp of ancient languages in order to exercise our God-given dominion over his creation as well as better understand the texts of Scripture in their original languages. See more on this further down.

be disciples of Christ *and* that it is okay for them to be disciples of the secular-humanist, state-sponsored curriculum. The two are at odds; and the state-sponsored language arts curriculum is, in principle, foundation, means, and goal, *against* our Lord Jesus Christ.

Chapter 5

Mathematics

WHEN IT COMES TO mathematics, generally people are a little more suspect of our beliefs. Surely there is no wrong way to teach mathematics, right? After all, it has to be the one neutral subject in our children's education, correct?

But we have already stated that all facts relate to the Lord Jesus Christ (Col 1:16–17, 2:3; Heb 1:2–3), and that whoever is not with him is, by definition and by default, against him (Matt 12:30). The case is no less true when it comes to mathematics.[1]

So again, we must ask even some basic questions:

- In the secular-humanist, state-sponsored curriculum, what is the foundation and goal of math?
- What is the purpose of math and what is the point in learning it?

Often we are told that our children need math in order to go about their day-to day-business. Without basic math, we could not productively go to the grocery store and know whether or not we have enough money to purchase the items in our shopping cart. Likewise, without advanced math we could not advance our

---

1. Again, here I must highly recommend Vern S. Poythress' *Redeeming Mathematics: A God-Centered Approach* for digging deeper into this topic.

technology for the human race (put a man on the moon; develop automatic air conditioning, etc.)

True enough. But true to the soul of the secular-humanist, state-sponsored curriculum, our great God and King is left completely out of the picture, even though it is from his very own grace that we have the ability to learn these things.

The ethic of gaining knowledge of math in the secular-humanist, state-sponsored curriculum is, of course, pragmatism. Our children should learn math because it is advantageous for them (or even the planet) to do so. So even at the start, whether it centers around ourselves or the planet, the curriculum takes no consideration of the God who created us or the planet (or even math, for that matter).

In contrast to that approach, according to Scripture our children are to be taught math in order to glorify God and serve others. We are to use our knowledge of math for our own home (Prov 31:16a), for the good of mankind (Lev 19:18b), and for the dominion *over* the planet (not servanthood *under* the planet, see Ps 8). But behind all this, the foundation and end goal of why we are to use our knowledge of math is to glorify God (1 Cor 10:31).

But to press the point even further, let us ask the question:

- What is the true foundation of math?

Since this is God's world, surely we ought to study it according to his rules. But the secular-humanist, state-sponsored curriculum discards his rulebook for knowledge and, instead of beginning with the fear of the Lord (Prov 1:7), it has man begin with himself. We are told that mathematics is a neutral field of thought on which we can depend regardless of our religion.

However, God says otherwise.

All the treasures of wisdom and knowledge are deposited in Christ (Col 2:3) and find their ultimate meaning in him (Col 1:16–17; Heb 1:3). To say at the outset that his lordship is irrelevant—even in the neutral field of mathematics—is to deny him his rightful role in our thought life.

Mathematics

For just a small example of how this plays out, let us return to our example in the introduction of this work. We agree with our secular-humanist fellow man that 2+2=4. But we are not at all in agreement with the foundation of that knowledge, nor the end goal for that knowledge.

The secular-humanist can say without hesitation that 2+2=4, today. But when pressed to answer how he *knows* that 2+2=4 will still be the case tomorrow he has to rely on faith—not on God—but on faith that the principles of mathematics won't change between today and tomorrow. He's not going to admit this though. He's going to say that it's just the case that two plus two will still equal four tomorrow, and that we must just accept it as a universal truth.

But this presents a problem for the secular-humanist: How does he know that 2+2=4 is a universal truth? In order to claim knowledge of a universal truth, one must either (a) have universal knowledge, (b) learn that truth from someone with universal knowledge, or (c) be claiming that knowledge on a blind, subjective leap of faith.

Let us examine these options in conjunction with the secular-humanist, state-sponsored curriculum. Will the one teaching from this curriculum have universal knowledge? Of course not.

Has the secular-humanist been everywhere in the universe? Even if he were somehow to get everywhere in the universe, he would still have a problem. How would he know that the second he left one part of the universe to travel to another, something hadn't changed in the realm of mathematics (or any matter of reality) in one of the previously visited parts of the universe? So, not only would he have to get to everywhere in the universe, he would have to *be* everywhere in the universe at the exact same time. But, it's still further complicated. Even if he were in the entire universe at the exact same time it still would not be enough to have universal knowledge. Because at the very second that he ceases to have that universal presence, his ability to have universal knowledge ceases too.

So, in this example, for a secular-humanist to claim knowledge of a universal truth (such as 2+2=4, or any other mathematical principle upon which we rely), he would have to be everywhere in the universe, at the same time, all of the time. There is only one man (John 1:14) we know who is able to do that (Col 1:16–17; Heb 1:3). But he is the very one that the secular-humanist, state-sponsored curriculum will not tolerate. And since that is the case, the idea of learning a universal truth *from someone who has universal knowledge*, is out of the question.

This leaves the secular-humanist, state-sponsored curriculum with one option: claim knowledge of a universal truth (that is, a truth that applies at all places at all times) simply on blind, subjective faith.

Now some might be thinking, how is this blind, subjective faith? Have we not seen in all our past experiences that two plus two has always equaled four? And if that is the case, is it not only logical to expect that to be the case in the future? Yet here is where we need to be careful with our use of the word "logic."

It is logical to expect that to be the case if someone who has universal knowledge has revealed that to us. But if we have negated that as an option at the outset (as the secular-humanist, state-sponsored curriculum has), then it is not logical at all. In order to know that a universal truth will take place in the future, one is relying on what is called the principle of induction—the belief that the future will behave like the past.

Gravity worked yesterday, and we expect it to work the same way tomorrow. The principles of algebra worked yesterday, and we expect them to work the same way tomorrow. However, just because we expect it to does not mean that it will happen. Now here is how the argument usually goes: "But in the past, the future has always been like the past; therefore, we should expect it to continue that way." But that is a fallacy. In the past, the future has always been like the past. But logically, that doesn't tell us anything about the future. It *only* tells us about the past. In order to know that *in the future* the future will still be behaving like the past, one would have to know the future. This takes us back to claiming knowledge of a universal truth.

Mathematics

So again, far from being neutral in regard to Jesus Christ, even at the *foundation* of mathematics and our reliance on mathematics to get us through the day or send us out of the earth's atmosphere, the secular-humanist, state-sponsored curriculum will lead our children away from being disciples of Christ and have them rather express a blind, subjective faith in the otherwise fallacious principle of induction.

Now, I say "otherwise," because as Christians our reliance on the principle of induction is not fallacious (nor blind or subjective). Obviously, we *do* believe that 2+2=4 is a universal truth and can be relied upon to make calculations today and tomorrow, and that, barring any miracles of God,[2] it will continue to be the case throughout history. But why do *we* believe that?

From the Christian perspective, we would say that it's because God created the universe in wisdom (Gen 1:1—2:1), establishing an order of how the universe will operate that reflects his own thought (Prov 8:12, 22–31) and proclaims his own glory (Ps 19:1–6). Two plus two equals four is a universal concept that God has created by his own wisdom, and it is the case, and can be counted on to be the case, because he has so ordained it and revealed to us that we can rely on the principle of induction for our thought patterns (see Gen 1:14, 8:22; cf. Ps 104:19; Luke 12:54–55).

In other words, 2+2=4 because God, who is everywhere in the universe at the same time, all the time, has created it that way, sustains it that way, and has revealed it to us.

Does that mean the secular-humanist, state-sponsored school teacher cannot teach 2+2=4? Well, no, he *can* teach it. But to the degree that he teaches it as something we just accept on blind faith rather than on faith in the Lord Jesus Christ to sustain 2+2=4 in the universe (Col 1:17; Heb 1:3), he certainly can't teach it rightly without deviating from the secular-humanist, state-sponsored curriculum. And while secular-humanists can, and do, and will use 2+2=4 and all other principles of mathematics—and even use

---

2. See John 6:9–14 to see how Jesus made five loaves of bread + two fish = enough food to feed over 5,000 people and still have twelve baskets leftover.

it well—all the while they cannot even give an account for why they are able to use it.

And why do they use it? Again, for pragmatic reasons.

Why are Christians commanded to rely on the universal principles God has set forth in his world? Because by doing so we are able to exercise our faith in him and in the promises he has made concerning the natural order of the universe. We are able, by his power, to have dominion over his creation. We are able to use 2+2=4 and all other principles and instances of mathematics (whether simple or complex) to glorify God and love our neighbor—the summary of our lives here on earth (Matt 22:37–40).

But would our children get that kind of discipleship from the secular-humanist, state-sponsored curriculum, even in the most allegedly neutral area of math? They would not. They would not even be given an adequate foundation for relying on math in the first place. And they would be given no morally good reason to use math; that is, they would not be told the purpose of math is to glorify God, by having dominion over the earth in service to the church and our neighbor.

As Christian parents, we would rather our children learn math and its principles based not on a blind faith, but on a well-lit faith (Ps 36:9; John 1:4) in the lordship of Jesus Christ, as a way of serving and loving him and our neighbors, and glorifying him in what he has created.

Chapter 6

Natural Sciences

It would be tedious to repeat all the above for this section. In short, the natural sciences curriculum relies just as much on the universal truths discussed above as does the mathematics curriculum. It has the same foundation of relying on these principles—on blind faith—purely out of conventional or pragmatic reasons. And the curriculum will not direct the use of science to the glory of God and as a way of loving one's neighbor. Rather, pragmatism rules the day yet again. It is with science that man has discovered how to end the life of a child before it is born into the world, and it is with the pragmatic approach to ethics combined with the fallen nature of man that this is seen as a good thing to do. Whether this is done surgically or pharmaceutically, this is not a way of loving our neighbors; and science learned in a Christian worldview would never point to such a horrendous goal. But science learned in a secular-humanist, state-sponsored curriculum will point to that position as a viable option, given the ethics that are taught from the science curriculum.

The trust in 2+2=4 is the same kind of trust in the behavior of electrons and protons, in the law of gravity, and in the other mathematical calculations on which much of science depends. Its foundation is the same for both: in secular-humanist, state-sponsored curriculum, it is illogically founded on nothing. In Christianity, it is rationally founded in the very creator and sustainer of all things visible and invisible (Col 1:16–17). In the secular-humanist, state-sponsored curriculum, the goal of science is utility. In Christianity, the goal of science is to glorify God by having dominion over his creation and loving our neighbors (including the unborn).

So we need not repeat ourselves.

The only real debate in this section not otherwise dealt with is the idea of macro-evolution in the field of biology. The problem here is that it is not science at all, but merely a philosophy of history.

Some might be very upset at hearing that, but it is the case nonetheless. If by science we mean a way of making observations in a controlled environment through repeatable tests so as to ascertain how the world works in a natural way, then macro-evolution just does not and cannot fit that mold.

No man here today was around "billions" of years ago to tell us what he has observed regarding the world then compared to now. And it's not as though men have been writing down their observations for even the *supposed* 200,000 years or so of man's history.

Yet, in the secular-humanist, state-sponsored curriculum, our children would be taught that man is not a direct creation of God but a life-form that has evolved over billions of years from a single-celled organism. Where is the proof? Where is the evidence at least? There is none.

Of course, our children wouldn't be told that there is no evidence. They would be given several forms of "evidence," each with the presuppositions of no God and billions of years *having* to be used in interpreting that evidence.[1] And though this is not science

---

1. We must keep in mind that this is in direct opposition to the word of God that death came as a result of sin. So we simply cannot have billions of years of death from all these pre-man life forms until we eventually get to man. Again, the secular-humanist, state-sponsored curriculum is not *neutral* in regard to Christ and his word; it is *against* him and his word. It would be impossible to cite all the references here for this information, but in general one can find a wealth of information on this topic from the following ministries and think tanks:

and is a form of philosophy of history, all the while this would not be presented to our children as something that can be debated as a matter of philosophy; but it would be presented to them as plain fact (and scientific fact at that). The obvious problem is that in Scripture, God alone is *the* One to be taken for granted in all of our thought (Prov 1:7). *He* is the inarguable fact of all of life (Isa 44:6; John 14:6).

Those discipled from a secular-humanist, state-sponsored curriculum will be told, at least implicitly if not outright explicitly, to forsake that God in their minds (a foolish endeavor to be sure—see Ps 14:1; cf. Prov 1:7). They will be taught from that curriculum to start first with the assumption that he does not exist, or perhaps that even if he does exist, man can think properly without relying first and foremost on his revelation.

We don't need to go any further here. This was Eve's mistake. Having been redeemed by the Lord Jesus Christ, we need not repeat it. And we certainly have an obligation to our children to teach them, through Christ's power, to overcome it (2 Cor 11:3; 1 Cor 10:13).

-*Answers in Genesis*
-*Biblical Science Institute*
-*Creation Ministries International*
-*The Institute for Creation Research*

Chapter 7

Social Sciences

Now we have arrived at the Social Sciences, usually comprised of history, geography, civics, etc. And so, as with the other subjects, we must ask, is there really a difference in learning these things from a Christian worldview than there is in learning them from an anti-Christian worldview?[1] Does the fact, "In fourteen hundred and ninety-two, Columbus sailed the ocean blue," really mean something significantly different when learned from a Christian point of view than from the secular-humanist, state-sponsored curriculum?

Of course, our answer is yes. But why?

Let us ask these general questions to get started:

- What is history? And is it knowable?
- If history can be known, can we know it before it becomes history?
- Is the history of man an account of his failures and successes, in cooperation with, or against, his fellow man? Or is it an account of his interactions with God and the rewards and consequences based on those interactions? Or is it both?

---

1. Again we say "anti-Christian" because that is what the Bible calls it when someone is not decidedly *with* Christ (Matt 12:30).

- Who controls history? Is it controlled by the free-will acts of man, or is it controlled by an all-powerful divine being?
- What is the purpose of learning history? And how do we evaluate it?

It is true these questions are not set up to be answered in a simple way. But the glaring problem is that the secular-humanist, state-sponsored curriculum will presume to know *the simple* answers to these questions and then teach them to our children.

The state-sponsored curriculum would have our children believe that history is simply the record of things in the past, according to reliable accounts that we have as interpreted by the experts of historical academia. In this curriculum, it will certainly not start with the eternally existing God creating the world (John 1:1–3), but with the cosmos coming into existence apart from him.

Further, in this curriculum, our children would be taught that history is knowable insofar as the records our children read are reliable and are interpreted according to the standards of the history experts in the world of academia.[2] All the while, the record we as Christians *know* to be reliable, and the very standard of reliability—the word of God—would be taught to our children as being inconsequential when dealing with history.

Is the study of man's history merely a study of man's thoughts and actions with his fellow man? Or is it a study of his interaction with God and God's interaction with him? The state-sponsored curriculum will not tolerate there being an all-powerful God who has divine sovereignty even over the free acts of man. There will be discussion with our children of man's *alleged* interactions with God (or other gods); but in the end, our children will be taught that historical fact is the account of man's *alleged* experience of God and *actual* experience in reality, as if the two are mutually exclusive.

The curriculum would further teach our children that since God does not control history, man does. The teaching that man

---

2. Although, as discussed previously, there is a part of history that really is not knowable, as it tends to be written by the winners.

controls his own destiny typically accompanies this line of thinking. Our children would be taught that the only thing stopping them from achieving all that they can is themselves. There is no God who has a plan of his own for them (regardless of their pursuits; see Prov 19:21); and there is no spiritual warfare in which they must engage (Eph 6:10–20). They would be discipled in the belief that only they can shape and master their own destinies, and that apart from the Lord Jesus Christ.

But finally, what is the purpose of our children learning all this? In the secular-humanist, state-sponsored curriculum, beyond the quip that, "Those who cannot remember the past are condemned to repeat it,"[3] our children would be taught that they should learn from the mistakes of others in history, and should build upon their successes.

Well, that part is certainly true. But it brings us to our final question: How do our children evaluate history? In a secular-humanist, state-sponsored curriculum, how would our children be taught to evaluate the Holocaust?[4] How would they be taught to evaluate the sexual revolution? How would they be taught to evaluate the Vietnam War, or the Gulf War, or the various abstract wars on poverty, drugs, and terror?

As parents (many of whom grew up in secular-humanist, state-sponsored schools), we instinctively know the answers to these questions, don't we?

The Holocaust was bad. The sexual revolution was good. The Vietnam War (even now) is a giant question mark. And do we think our children will be given any other type of answer?

Maybe they will; but the problem is that they still wouldn't be given the tools to actually evaluate history for themselves. How are they to learn from the mistakes of others and build upon their

---

3. This quote, or derivations of it, is generally attributed to George Santayana.

4. Keep in mind that all along our children would have been taught the ethics of utility. And then bear in mind that Adolf Hitler saw *the final solution* of completely eliminating the Jews as the best that could be done for mankind (i.e., pragmatic ethics).

successes, if they aren't taught how to think through the issues that the others before them faced?

So, what is the Christian response? Scripture, of course.

According to Scripture, history, as the account of all things past, *can* be known and should be known (Deut 8:11-18; cf. Jer 6:16). And though the history of the *world* starts with the divine creation of the physical universe (Gen 1:1), and the history of *man* starts on the sixth day of that creation (Gen 1:31), there was a time when the world was not, but God was (John 1:1-3; cf. Ps 90:2). But from the time of man's creation, history has been and will be an account, not only of man's dealings with his fellow man (Gen 1:27) and the rest of God's created order (Gen 2:15-20), but also with man's actual dealings with God (Gen 2:19, 3:6, 6:5, 12:4) and God's actual dealings with man (Gen 2:7, 2:16-17, 3:17-19; 6:5-22; 12:1-3, 15:6, 17-21).

Because this same God declares the end from the beginning (Isa 46:8-11), history can not only be known, but it can be known before it becomes history (John 14:29). Furthermore, because God is sovereign over all things (Matt 10:29; Rom 9:10-24), he alone is in complete control of history, using the free acts of man to accomplish all his holy will (Deut 32:39; 1 Sam 2:6-7; Isa 45:1-7; Dan 4:34-35; Acts 4:24-28).

As Christians, our children *are* to learn from history, in taking the lives of the faithful as an example (Rom 15:4; Heb 12:1-2) and the lives of the unfaithful as a warning (1 Cor 10:11-12). But their evaluation of their lives must be based on the authoritative word of God. How do our children evaluate the Holocaust, the Vietnam War, the sexual revolution, the Gulf War, the various abstract wars, and everything else in history—including Columbus's voyage to the Americas? They evaluate them in light of Scripture.

Concerning this, taking all of Jesus' commands to the ends of the earth so that the knowledge of the Lord will be as the waters cover the seas (Matt 28:18-20; cf. Hab 2:14; Isa 11:9), means his just laws and righteous ways go along with his disciples (Mic 4:1-5; Isa 2:2-4; cf. Heb 2:2; Isa 42:1). Therefore, when evaluating cultural or military events in history, the Scriptures are integral in determining the rights and wrongs of what has happened. Not only so, but they are just as significant in directing us even now in how society should live and how law should be applied. Our children ought to learn these things.

It should be noted briefly that learning geography goes with the territory of learning history. It would be almost impossible to learn history without learning geography. Not only that, but our Lord created the whole world and everything in it (Ps 24:1). And as the cultural mandate (Gen 1:28) has tasked us and our children with having dominion, and the Great Commission (Matt 28:18–20) has tasked us and our children with contributing to reaching the ends of the world, it would be good to know the physical layout of that domain.

Finally, does history have an ultimate purpose? Is there something in which history will finally have a resting point?

In the secular-humanist, state-sponsored curriculum, it is not known when history will end. But what would often be instructed to our children is that mankind will eventually be wiped out when the sun loses its power or some other galactic catastrophe happens, or when man destroys the planet himself either through war or through some other man-centered act.[5]

Yet again, if we allowed our children to be taught this idea of history, we would be allowing them to be disciples of secular-humanism rather than disciples of Jesus Christ. Our Lord, the interpreter of history himself (Isa 41:22) has told us that the world—as we know it—*will* come to an end. But this end will not be one of man's doing, but of God's (Isa 65:17; cf. 2 Pet 3:7; Rev 21:1). Yet, man's history will go on; and this too, not because man is going to figure out how to live forever, but because God has so declared that certain men will live in an everlasting destruction (Dan 12:2), while those who put their faith in his Son as the payment for their

---

5. Currently the consideration is *climate change* (formerly known as *global warming*). Regardless of one's stance on whether or not this is a genuine issue and, if so, if it is caused by humans, the Bible teaches that humans will not be able to cause so much damage that they will be able to destroy the earth themselves. It will be clearly and unmistakably the work of God (see 2 Pet 3:10).

sins (1 John 2:1–2) will live with him forever (Heb 9:27–28; cf. Rom 8:37–39).

Regardless, the history of man on the planet as we know it now *will* find its end in all bowing the knee to the Lord Jesus Christ (Phil 2:9–11), as all of history is summed up in him (Eph 1:9, 10). It is to this that all history points; and it is a hope and repose to which we and our children should look forward.

To have a true Christian education in history, our children must learn all of these basic things as being centered in Christ and his word; but if we have them discipled by the secular-humanist, state-sponsored curriculum, they will learn none of them. And again, by having them discipled by the secular-humanist, state-sponsored curriculum, we will not simply be neglecting to actively further make them disciples of Christ, but we will be *actively* furthering their discipleship away from him and into state-sponsored, secular-humanism. So, again, it does us well to bear this in mind:

> Temptations to sin are sure to come, but woe to the one through whom they come! It would be better for him if a millstone were hung around his neck and he were cast into the sea than that he should cause one of these little ones to sin. (Luke 17:1–2)

Chapter 8

Creative Arts

FINALLY, WE REACH PERHAPS the most often misunderstood subject in the secular-humanist, state-sponsored curriculum: the *creative* arts. Within this branch of knowledge we usually speak of visual art, music, poetry, drama, dance, etc. And as appealing as these arts can be, they are usually the first to go when budgets are cut in the state-sponsored curriculum.

As homeschooling parents, committed to a Christian worldview, that is fine in our estimation. Though, as seen above, since all the other departments of education are just as opposed, in principle, to the lordship of Jesus Christ, we would probably be just as fine if any of them were the first to go in budget cuts.

However, at this point in the book, what difference does this really make?

But of course, that's the question we need to ask, isn't it? As with all the other subjects in the secular-humanist, state-sponsored curriculum, what is the foundation and goal of the creative arts? Should it have any priority over the other areas of knowledge studied in state-sponsored curriculum? Or should it at least be *equal* to them? We know the answer here.

No, not in a secular-humanist, state-sponsored curriculum. And why is that? Because again, pragmatism is the ruling principle of the day. While Hollywood stars as a whole make a lot more money than an average chemical engineer, the likelihood of any one student in a typical government school becoming such a Hollywood star is drastically small compared to one becoming an engineer. And our children have to grow up to do *something*.[1] So the creative arts, being the least pragmatic, are generally the first to go.

Thankfully, in Christian education at home, we really don't have to worry about that being the case. But the question still remains for us: Are the creative arts on par with the other areas of education when it comes to knowledge of God's creation and our obligation to subdue it and have dominion?

And here, we as Christians answer with a resounding yes!

That might sound very odd at first. Surely, math and science, etc., are more important for us to learn than art, are they not? We might be tempted to think that; but, as in the cases above, in order to answer this question rightly we must turn to the Scriptures. The pragmatic temptation will have us ask questions like, "Has a picture ever cured cancer?" or, "Was it a song that enabled us to put a man on the moon?" But we might be surprised to see the importance that the Scriptures place on the creative arts.

Yes, God shows throughout his word how he has used the knowledge of math and science that he has given to men in order to build up the world throughout the generations (Gen 4:22; 1 Kgs 5:6, 6:10; 2 Chr 32:2–4). But for just a small sampling, let us also look at what things are described in undoubtedly positive light as being aesthetically beautiful in Scripture:

- The Lord himself (Ps 27:4)
- The city of God (Ps 50:2)
- The temple of God (Ps 96:6; cf. Rev 4:2–11)
- The feet of the messenger who brings good news of God (Isa 52:7)
- The people of God (Isa 62:3; cf. 1 Pet 2:6–10; Eph 2:19–22)

---

1. To which we agree; but as seen throughout, what our children do should be for the glory of God and the love of their neighbors.

- The clothing of the people of God (Exod 28:2, 40; cf. Is. 52:1; cf. Rev 19:8)

Not to mention, the garden of Eden and even the very angels to watch over it (Ezek 28:12–14) are described as among the most beautiful creations until the fulfillment of the new heavens and new earth (cf. Rev 21:19–26). Music, being a form of worship in itself, is held in high regard (Psalms 1–150) and even used for therapy (1 Sam 16:14–23); dancing is often a form of worship (Exod 15:20; 2 Sam 6:14; Ps 149:3, 150:4); and even drama is performed as a way of communicating God's truth to others (Ezek 4:1–3).

Furthermore, it is important for us to remember that the plans for the tabernacle/temple given to Moses were instructed to be completed by the most skillful craftsmen in the camp so that they might "devise *artistic* designs" (Exod 31:1–11, emphasis mine) for the meeting place between God and man.

The striking thing in the Scriptures about the creative arts is that they are never mentioned as a second-class form of knowledge. Daniel was well known for his mastery of the sciences (Dan 1:3–6, 17–19) while Ezekiel was equally known for his singing ability (Ezek 33:32). And David, himself a prophet of God, was known as the sweet singer of Israel (2 Sam 23:1).

In a Christian worldview, we ought to see visual art, music, poetry, drama, dance, etc., as being *just as valuable* in exercising our obligation to the cultural mandate as our work in science, math, literature, history, etc. It's no wonder that when we see the progress of the cultural mandate being recorded in Scripture, we see them together (Gen 2:20–21; Exod 35:30—36:1).

So then, what do we make of the use of the creative arts in a Christian worldview? Obviously the creative arts are important (as demonstrated above), but to what end? It's to the same end as all the other forms of knowledge. We use the creative arts to glorify God and serve our neighbors. And we teach our children to do the same.

But again, this is not remotely close to what the secular-humanist, state-sponsored curriculum will teach to our children about the creative arts. The purpose of the creative arts in the secular-humanist, state-sponsored curriculum is to glorify and serve one's self. And the curriculum will teach our children that art is meant to be a form of self-expression to which others must submit if they are to truly understand it.

Art from a Christian perspective, however, is meant to be a form of image-bearing expression through which one can glorify God and serve others, by demonstrating, in a creative fashion, a truth of God or his creation, or a truth of the human condition and how to respond. Whether we paint a picture, write a story, dramatize an act, play a song, dance a dance, this is what we are doing when we engage in the creative arts. And we do it all to represent God's truth in a beautiful and dynamic way to glorify him and love and serve our neighbors. Therefore, this is what we will teach our children concerning the creative arts and how to use them. They are not meant to have others bow to us. They are meant for us to add beauty and creativity to the world in service to others for the glory of God.[2]

In short, we use the creative arts as any other form of knowledge, to be better disciples of the Lord Jesus Christ. But our children will not receive that kind of discipleship regarding the creative arts (if there even is a program for them) in the secular-humanist, state-sponsored curriculum. Therefore, we will teach our children at home.

---

2. There is a terrific, brief article, "Hospitality and the Holy Imagination" that more powerfully illustrates this point here: https://readaloudrevival.com/zach-franzen/.

Conclusion

> "Whoever walks with the wise becomes wise,
> but the companion of fools will suffer harm."
> —PROVERBS 13:20

On the one hand, the struggle is completely understandable. State-sponsored education with a secular-humanist curriculum has been the norm for quite some time, and for decades has been accepted as a given in our culture. But on the other hand, when confronted with God's word and what it has to say about the parental obligation in raising our children (regardless of culture), it is difficult to justify sending our children to be discipled by an anti-Christian curriculum for (at least) thirteen years of their lives.

Why do *we* homeschool our children?

Because our responsibility as parents is not to have them become disciples of secular-humanism or the secular-humanist, state-sponsored curriculum. Our responsibility as parents is to raise our children up, day-in and day-out, from when they rise up to when they go to bed, to be disciples of the Lord Jesus Christ. Our responsibility is to ensure that whatever they learn, they learn it (as far as they can) in its right relation to Jesus Christ and his lordship.

Conclusion

This means that whatever they learn, their learning begins with the fear of the Lord (Prov 1:7). This means that whatever they learn, they recognize that it's only through his lordship they're able to learn it (Col 1:16–17, 29). This means that whatever they learn, they do so in order to glorify God (1 Cor 10:31) and love their neighbors (Luke 10:27).

Will any one of these things be taught in the secular-humanist, state-sponsored curriculum? Absolutely not. The secular-humanist, state-sponsored curriculum will begin their thinking with man rather than God (Gen 3:2–3, 6; cf. Isa 2:22), will not recognize the Lord as the very means from which they're able to learn anything at all (Job 32:8; cf. Dan 4), and will not give him the glory that is due him (Rom 1:21).

The Bible declares that a belief system that starts off with the assumption that there is no God, is foolish: "The fool says in his heart, 'There is no God'" (Ps 14:1). The entire secular-humanist, state-sponsored curriculum is based on that premise. The Bible further tells us to avoid such close connections with those who advocate such a belief system, whom it calls fools (Ps 1:1; Prov 13:20; 1 Cor 15:33; 2 Cor 6:14–18).

Furthermore, the Bible tells us that there is no neutral territory when it comes to the question of the Lord Jesus Christ. He says explicitly, "Whoever is not with me is against me" (Matt 12:30). So, if all the treasures of wisdom and knowledge find their true meaning in him (Col 2:3), because he is in fact Lord over all (Col 1:16–17; Heb 1:3; cf. Matt 28:28), and our children are taught that facts can be facts whether or not Jesus is Lord, they are being taught not to be *neutral* in regard to our Lord Jesus Christ, but to be *against* him.

Finally, if we ourselves are to pray, "Father . . . lead us not into temptation," (Matt 6:13) and then we send our children to be discipled by the above kind of curriculum that is purposed to set our children *against* the lordship of Christ, then we above all, are not only hypocritical in our prayer life, but are indeed cursed if our children should succumb to that temptation (Luke 17:1–2; Matt 18:6).

Education *is* discipleship. Our children can either be discipled by a secular-humanist, state-sponsored curriculum, or they can be discipled by their Christian parents at home, who will, as best they can (in the power of the Spirit—Col 1:29), bring them up to be disciples of the Lord Jesus Christ.

We opt for the latter. This is our calling as parents. And *this* is why we homeschool.

If you see it the way we do, our hope is that the question "Why do you homeschool?" will no longer be directed to us, but that rather it should be directed to Christians *who have the option to do so and don't*: "Why *aren't* you homeschooling?"

We pray that they would start.

> Everyone when he is fully trained *will be* like his teacher . . . (Luke 6:40, emphasis mine)

Appendix A

How Our Children Will Develop Socially

WE TEND TO THINK this question about how our children will develop socially when *not* put in a state-sponsored school (or even private school for that matter) is just kind of funny.

Clearly the common phrase, "kids these days," and other turns of phrase that are used to talk about the manner in which kids *don't* socialize properly (or even know what manners are, let alone use them) is evidence enough that the current system we use to socialize our children—or rather develop them socially—is not really working that well.

But allow us to be more specific.

The social development that goes on in secular-humanist, state-sponsored schools is not actually social development, as in making sure the capacity and ability of one's social skills is rising at an adequate pace relative to their language skills. We really see social impediment or stagnation at best. This is not a slight to public school teachers. All we are doing here is taking into account the very nature of children. They are, in fact, childish by nature (Eph 4:14).

If we take twenty children and have them teach each other, they're going to all learn how to be more and more like children. If we put one adult in the room there will be some level of discipline

How Our Children Will Develop Socially

in the atmosphere, but the children themselves will still behave like children. They will take social cues from their fellow classmates, and they will still see their classmates as principle teachers when it comes to how to interact with others.

This is not developing socially. This is developing childishly.

And while we do have a great love for the solid, private Christian schools out there that are available as an alternative to the state-sponsored schools, we see the problem as being the same. Please understand that we see it to a much lesser degree in such schools. This is not because the children are any less childish though. It's because many of them are regenerated by the Lord (1 John 5:1–5). And though still childish because of their nature of being children (Eph 4:14), they have the Holy Spirit in them removing their sin nature bit by bit (2 Cor 3:18).

It's also because the teachers have much more authority in their classrooms than their secular-humanist, state-sponsored counterparts. And this is not because they run their classrooms as dictators, but because their authority as teachers is derived from the word of God (Luke 6:40). And this foundation is emphasized throughout the program. God is the supreme and ultimate authority in all things (Isa 45:5–7), and it is to him we must submit in all things—even through his lesser rulers whom he has set in place over us (Eph 6:1, 5–8; Titus 3:1; 1 Pet 2:13–15).

Nonetheless, though acting in place of the parents (*in loco parentis*), these teachers are not the actual parents of the children; and because of the nature of children, they will not be seen as having the same authority as the children's own parents. And though many of their peers will be more sanctified when it comes to developing socially, they will still be children. And we would rather our children not take their cues from them in a setting that lends itself so easily for them to do so.

However, it *is* important for children to be able to engage with others their own age. So, the question is how will ours do so if we're homeschooling? Well, homeschooling doesn't mean we never leave the home. We certainly have them engaging with children their own age. This is done at church, at the playground, at the library—really at any place where there are other kids. However, the difference is that we (or several other adults at the same time) are overseeing their interactions. They are not left alone with a class of twenty some kids and one adult for many hours a week.

Furthermore, because social development is important to us, we will not be satisfied with our children merely learning how to talk to their peers. If we think about it, when in all of the rest of life other than a modern classroom setting are humans interacting with other humans that are for the most part the exact same age, and at similiar physical, mental, and emotional development stages as everyone else around them?

The workforce is not like that. The world of commerce is not like that. The neighborhoods are not like that. The churches are not like that. And homes are not like that. And yet—rightly so— we expect a socially developed person to be able to interact in all those types of communities. So, what do we do as homeschooling parents to develop our children socially? We expose them to those places and show by example and experience how to interact.

We take our children to our workplaces (when allowed and appropriate). We take them shopping or to run errands. We take them around our neighborhood. We take them to church. And we teach them how to interact with people in these various venues, not just with the children but also with the adults, the way we do: "Hello, how are you?" "Thank you," "Have a nice day," etc.

Now, we recognize that not everyone has the same social temperament. Some are definitely more extroverted, by nature, while others are more introverted. However, even the introverted among us are able to interact in their own way with all sorts of people in a variety of settings. And we believe that our duty as parents is to disciple our children in being disciples of the Lord Jesus Christ, teaching them how to interact with others so as to best love their neighbor (Luke 10:27).

And if that's the case, we think it's clear from the above discussion that the best way to do that is for their social development to be overseen by those who love them most (us) and are able to best expose them to the most variety of social situations (again, us).

Appendix B

Homeschooling Versus Private Christian Schooling

THERE IS A VERY real part of me that has nothing against private Christian schooling. That is, if the Christian school were to teach all things it teaches according to God's word as the standard and relate everything back to the lordship of Christ (as very limitedly outlined above), then it would be hard to dissuade others from sending their children there.

On the practical level there are certainly many pluses. One of them is the division of labor. At a private Christian school, the literature, mathematics, natural sciences, social sciences, and creative arts teachers will all be more specialized in their respective fields than a typical mother or father at home. It also, in many cases, frees one or both of the parents up, timewise, to do other things that they otherwise might not be able to do: make more capital for the home, serve at church, volunteer in parachurch organizations, better keep up with housework, write a book! There are other pluses to be sure.

However, there are also several things that homeschooling offers that even a private, Christian school cannot. For one thing, the social development as stated above (Appendix A). What is more to us, though, is the idea of discipleship. Certainly discipleship can be done through someone other than parents. After all, the church is commissioned to make disciples of all nations (Matt 28:18–20). But as stated previously in this work, we believe that for parents, the disciple-making should start at home. If we are not willing to train our own children (ourselves—Deut 6:1–7) to be disciples of Christ, what does that say to them by the example we are setting (Matt 7:20)?

Even in the New Testament we observe an interesting phenomenon. While the apostle Paul never spoke ill of his parents, and simultaneously always instructed children to obey theirs (Eph 6:1–3; Col 3:20), he never mentions his parents in a positive light either. He never mentions how he was discipled by them or whether or not they were even believers.

Instead, he mentions his private schooling (Acts 22:3). The interesting thing about his private schooling though is that it served as an impetus not for him to know God better, but simply to be better than his peers and impress his teachers, being zealous for their traditions (Gal 1:14; cf. Acts 5:34). This is not at all to say these are the kind of graduates private Christian schools are turning out in our day, but it is interesting to see that these were Paul's motives in a school-type environment.

Meanwhile, when he writes to Timothy, he clearly lays out the multigenerational discipleship of the family: "I am reminded of your sincere faith, a faith that dwelt first in your grandmother Lois and your mother Eunice and now, I am sure, dwells in you as well" (2 Tim 1:5). And again, if our primary purpose in being parents is to raise our children to be disciples of the Lord Jesus Christ, then what better way to do that than to be teaching them ourselves, day in and day out (Deut 6:1-7)?

Some might here say that their desire is to raise their children to be disciples of Jesus Christ day in and day out; but the best way they see that being done is through private Christian education. We don't really have an argument *against* that other than the following.

While there might be a better division of labor and other pluses in private, Christian education, we do believe there is wisdom in God's word wanting the parents—for whatever reason—to be the primary disciplers of their children (Deut 6:1–7). We think there really is something to the idea of children seeing how their parents go about the day-to-day business of work, errands, commerce, household chores, church, and all the other daily living tasks that they might not otherwise be exposed to when in a modern school setting.

Our hope is that our children will become fully mature disciples of our Lord Jesus Christ. Clearly there are always exceptions, but we think the way God intends that to happen as a normal course of action is for them to see how we live out our lives in his grace throughout all the areas of our lives. This simply cannot be done if they're in a classroom, away from us, five days a week.

However, out of all the sections of this book, this is the one we hold to the most loosely. As stated previously, while these reasons are our own for preferring homeschooling over private, Christian education, we certainly wouldn't try to dissuade anyone from sending their children to a private Christian school—at least one that sees education generally outlined in the way it is in this work, with Christ being the foundation, means, and goal of all education and every fact being related back to him.

Appendix C

A Special Note to My Friends Involved in Government Schools

To my brothers and sisters in Christ—whether faculty, staff, or parents—working in or sending your children to government schools:

Please know that I understand the importance of taking care of the material needs of your family (Prov 13:22; 2 Cor 12:14; 1 Tim 5:8). I recognize that for many—even if you agree with everything written in this book—it just isn't economically feasible to both homeschool your children (or send your children to a private Christian school) *and* pay the bills. And if you're in that position, it reminds me of you being in a *similar* position as the parents of Daniel. They didn't have a choice either. They *had* to let their son be educated by the Babylonian government (Dan 1:1–6). Now of course, it's slightly different. You don't have to let them attend these schools on pain of death. But you do have to if you want to be able to pay your bills, put food on the table, and clothe yourselves and your children.[1]

---

1. Of course, on the biblical side of economics and the free-market economy it espouses (Exod 20:6), it would be prudent to fight for the state to stop the secular-humanist, state-sponsored education altogether. If we all were able to keep more of our income rather than have it sent to state-sponsored schools (either through our property taxes or funneled through other taxes), then we

A Special Note to My Friends Involved in Government Schools

Or, if you're working for state-sponsored schools in order to provide for your family, and there is no real alternative for you at this point (I realize many private, Christian schools just do not pay enough to live on), I understand the need (for the time) to stay working for government schools (just as Daniel, when he was older, *had* to work for that government—Dan 6:1–3).

To you all, I am saying that I understand your situation, and my heart goes out to you. And until our Lord provides such an opportunity for you, I pray for you and encourage you to continue to be a light in the darkness. But also I pray that you will pray for and look for an opportunity to leave this situation so that your children can be discipled the way our Lord intends and/or so that you can provide for your family in a more satisfying way.

> For the LORD hears the needy
> and does not despise his own people who are prisoners.
> (Ps 69:33)

To my brothers and sisters in Christ who have the *option* to disciple their children at home (or at least send them to a private Christian school) *or* work at a private school, but for whatever reason, maintain your relationship with the government schools: I love you just as much, but I only ask that you hear me on the following points:

I know that your desire either to educate the students sent to your state-sponsored classrooms, or to have your own children educated in those state-sponsored classrooms, is a godly desire. And I know your heart must resonate with the apostle John when he wrote, "I have no greater joy than to hear that my children are walking in the truth" (3 John 1:4). For surely that is precisely what you are trying to teach all of your students or to have all your children learn—the truth!

But here is where we must know that the current secular-humanist, state-sponsored system in which the children are placed is, at its core, anti-Christian and thus anti-truth. Since Christ is

---

would be able to better provide for our families and possibly not need two incomes so that we could more easily homeschool our children.

himself "the truth" (John 14:6), and the secular-humanist, state-sponsored school system has so blatantly rejected the Lord Jesus Christ at the very outset of its educating principles, then the system in which you work, or in which your children are taught, is truly anti-Christian. That being the case, taken in conjunction with all that has been said in the book (which, if you haven't read yet, I encourage you to), I write to the following:

To the *teachers* (and the administrative staff supporting those roles) who have an option *not* to be involved in the government schools, but are:

Yes, you may be a wonderful exception to the system. You may endeavor to teach your students the truth about reality (that man is by nature a sinner, rebellious toward God, and in desperate need to turn to the only Savior for salvation and sanctification—Eph 2:1–10), about knowledge (that true knowledge at its very foundation can only be found in and based in the one living and true God—Prov 1:7; Col 2:3), and about ethics (that the only one who has the authority to determine what is right and wrong and who will at the end bring all into judgment is the one living and true God; and so allegiance in ethical matters must be to him and him alone—Gen 18:25; Deut 32:4; Job 8:3, 34:10; Isa 5:20; Ps 51:4; Eccl 12:13-14; Dan 12:2; Rev 20:11–15, 22:12). No matter what your role in the school, these things will be brought to bear on your subject matter and your interactions with the students.

But surely you know that at whatever point you teach these wonderful truths, you are teaching contrary to the very nature and desires of your employer: the secular-humanist government that desires you to *only* teach the secular-humanist curriculum. And you must ask yourselves, is that truly right according to God's word (see Col 3:22)?

Perhaps you see yourself as a missionary laboring in the mission field, similar to those who are in covert situations in foreign parts of the world. And would that your missionary work be fruitful! But I would then ask you to also consider, if this truly is *missionary* work, how is it funded? Is it funded by the church, through freewill offerings, which is the scriptural support for funding

A SPECIAL NOTE TO MY FRIENDS INVOLVED IN GOVERNMENT SCHOOLS

missionary work (see 3 John 1:7–8)? Or is it funded by the state through the coercive power of taxation? So I ask you to consider, is it right for you or anybody else to pay taxes (through coercion) for a system that denies the lordship of Christ for the sake of you and a few other brave and noble exceptions to carry out your *missionary work in education*?[2]

I would say there is no place in Scripture where we can find biblical support for that way of doing missionary work (again, see 3 John 1:7–8). And so, I ask you to take that wonderful desire and passion you have to teach students the truth—take it and use it (again, if you are economically able) with your very own children, or if need be in the private market, receiving your income from ones who are in line with your own Christian values about truth, reality, knowledge, and ethics.

To the *parents* who have the option *not* to be involved in the government schools, but are:

I know it is not easy and probably not even socially acceptable for some of you to take your children out of government schools. And I know many of you might feel like you're completely ill-equipped and unprepared to homeschool your children. However, I ask you to consider that that is only what the culture is saying to you. God says you are equipped and are prepared by virtue of you being their parents (Deut 6:4–7).

---

2. One of my good friends was kind enough to point out to me to be careful here.

He remarked: "Couldn't this argument be applied to a lesser degree to anyone who works in an industry funded by taxes? Defense contractors? Postal workers? Members of the military? For any Christian who works in a taxpayer-funded industry, there is an element where their values do not align with the secular government. Should they then not work in that industry?"

This is certainly a valid point, and I think this question deserves its day at the debate table. But the point I'm raising here (as opposed to defense contractors, postal workers, etc.) is that education is a distinct field altogether (and the one in which this entire work is focused). Regardless, the argument I usually get is that Christian teachers see themselves as missionaries to the children. That argument is not generally raised in regard to defense contractors, postal workers, etc.

A Special Note to My Friends

Not only that, but consider that the government school system *is* discipling your children. From the very beginning, your children are taught at worst, to deny the lordship of Christ at the outset, and at best that his lordship is irrelevant. Is that what the Scriptures teach? Certainly not (Ps 14:1; Prov 1:7; 1 Cor 1:18–21; Col 2:3, 8–10).

And so, you now have the double duty to undo everything that the government schools are teaching your children, and then to rebuild their education on the Rock foundation of Jesus Christ (Matt 7:24–27; cf. Deut 32:4; 1 Cor 10:4). Wouldn't it be much simpler on them and you, and more closely aligned with Scripture, if they just learned from you at the outset?[3]

So, I plead with you: if you haven't read this small work, please consider it—or any of the works in the bibliography. But *most importantly*, read the Scriptures themselves concerning education; and in *their light* (Ps 36:9), consider these things, pray about them, and see if they aren't so.

> Whoever ignores instruction despises himself,
> but he who listens to reproof gains intelligence.
> The fear of the LORD is instruction in wisdom,
> and humility comes before honor.
> (Prov 15:32–33)

---

3. Some see their *children* as missionaries. But we must always remember that according to Scripture children are not yet ready for missionary work. They are, by nature, "tossed to and fro by the waves and carried about by every wind of doctrine" (Eph 4:14).

The secular-humanist, state-sponsored schools are not missionary grounds for our children. They are seedbeds for temptation. And we know what our Lord says about sending our children into temptation: "Temptations are sure to come, but woe to the one through whom they come! It would be better for him if a millstone were hung around his neck and he were cast into the sea than that he should cause one of these little ones to sin" (Luke 17:1, 2; cf. Matt 18:6).

So we must consider how great of a sin is it, if our responsibility is to disciple them from sunrise to sunset in knowing the Lord and his commands, but instead we send them to be discipled by a curriculum that constantly tempts them to ignore and reject the lordship of Christ at every turn?

Bibliography

Bahnsen, Greg L. "A Thousand Generations" Basic Training Series. Covenant Media Foundation. Audio recording. http://www.cmfnow.com/athousandgenerations.aspx.

———. "Why Johnny Can't Pray." Covenant Media Foundation. Audio recording. http://www.cmfnow.com/hotpotatoes.aspx.

Basham, Patrick, et al. *Home Schooling: From the Extreme to the Mainstream*. 2nd ed. Studies in Education Policy. https://www.fraserinstitute.org/sites/default/files/Homeschooling2007.pdf

Baucham, Voddie, Jr., dir. *The Children of Caesar*. Powder Springs, GA: American Vision, 2007, DVD.

Berkhof, Louis, and Cornelius Van Til. *Foundations of Christian Education: Addresses to Christian Teachers*. Phillipsburg, NJ: P&R, 1990.

Blumenfeld, Samuel L. *Is Public Education Necessary?* Powder Springs, GA: American Vision, 2011.

Callihan, Wesley, et al. *Classical Education and the Homeschool*. Moscow: Canon, 2001.

Clark, Gordon Haddon. *A Christian Philosophy of Education*. Unicoi, TN: The Trinity Foundation, 2000.

Dabney, Robert Lewis. *On Secular Education*. Moscow: Canon, 1996.

DeMar, Gary. *Whoever Controls the Schools Rules the World*. Powder Springs, GA: American Vision, 2007.

D'Escoto, David, and Kim D'Escoto. *The Little Book of Big Reasons to Homeschool*. Nashville: B&H, 2007.

Ferenstein, Gregory. "Why Google Doesn't Care about College Degrees, in 5 Quotes." https://venturebeat.com/2014/04/25/why-google-doesnt-care-about-college-degrees-in-5-quotes.

Frame, John M. *Salvation Belongs to the Lord: An Introduction to Systematic Theology*. Phillipsburg, NJ: P&R, 2006.

Franzen, Zach. "Hospitality and the Holy Imagination." https://readaloudrevival.com/zach-franzen.

Bibliography

Gaebelein, Frank E. *The Pattern of God's Truth: The Integration of Faith and Learning.* Winona Lake, IN: BMH, 1985.

Gatto, John Taylor. *Dumbing Us Down: The Hidden Curriculum of Compulsory Schooling.* Gabriola Island, BC: New Society, 2005.

———. *The Underground History of American Education: An Intimate Investigation Into the Prison of Modern Schooling, Volume 1.* New York: Oxford Scholars, 2017.

———. *Weapons of Mass Instruction: A School Teacher's Journey through the Dark World of Compulsory Schooling.* Gabriola Island, BC: New Society, 2009.

Gunn, Colin, and Joaquin Fernandez, dirs. *IndoctriNation: Public Schools and the Decline of Christianity in America.* Waco, TX: Gunn Productions. 2011.

Gunn, Colin, and Joaquin Fernandez. *IndoctriNation: Public Schools and the Decline of Christianity.* Green Forest, AR: Master, 2012.

Ham, Ken, and Brit Beemer. *Already Gone: Why Your Kids Will Quit Church and What You Can Do to Stop it.* Green Forest, AR: Master, 2009.

Hebbard, Aaron B., ed. *95 Theses for a New Reformation: For the Church on the 500th Anniversary of the Reformation.* Eugene, OR: Resource, 2017.

Hudson, Paul. "100 Top Entrepreneurs Who Succeeded Without a College Degree." https://www.elitedaily.com/news/business/100-top-entrepreneurs-succeeded-college-degree.

Machen, J. Gresham. *Education, Christianity, and the State.* Unicoi, TN: The Trinity Foundation, 2004.

McCluskey, Neal P. *Feds in the Classroom: How Big Government Corrupts, Cripples, and Compromises American Education.* Lanham, MD: Rowman & Littlefield, 2007.

Moore, E. Ray, Jr. *Let My Children Go: Why Parents Must Remove their Children from Public Schools Now.* Columbia, SC: Gilead Media, 2002.

North, Gary, ed. *Foundations of Christian Scholarship: Essays in the Van Til Perspective.* Vallecito, CO: Ross House, 2001.

Perks, Stephen C. *The Christian Philosophy of Education Explained.* Whitby, UK: Avant, 1992.

Poythress, Vern S. *Redeeming Mathematics: A God-Centered Approach.* Wheaton, IL: Crossway, 2015.

Reynolds, Glenn Harlan. *The K-12 Implosion.* New York: Encounter, 2013.

Ryken, Philip Graham. *Art for God's Sake.* Phillipsburg, NJ: P&R, 2006.

Rushdoony, Rousas John. *Intellectual Schizophrenia.* Vallecito, CO: Ross House, 2002.

———. *The Messianic Character of American Education.* Vallecito, CO: Ross House, 1963.

———. *The Mythology of Science.* Vallecito: Ross House Books, 2001.

Schaeffer, Francis A. *Art and the Bible.* Downers Grove, IL: Intervarsity, 1973.

Shortt, Bruce N. *The Harsh Truth about Public Schools.* Vallecito, CO: Chalcedon, 2007.

BIBLIOGRAPHY

Smale, Thomas. "8 Hugely Successful People Who Didn't Graduate College." https://www.entrepreneur.com/article/249683.

Sproul, R. C., Jr. *When You Rise Up: A Covenantal Approach to Homeschooling.* Phillipsburg, NJ: P&R, 2004.

Swanson, Kevin. *The Second Mayflower.* Parker, CO: Generations with Vision, 2008.

Sykes, Charles J. *Fail U.: The False Promise of Higher Education.* New York: St. Martin's, 2016.

Van Til, Cornelius. *Essays on Christian Education.* Phillipsburg, NJ: P&R, 1979.

Veith, Gene Edward. *State of the Arts: From Bezalel to Mapplethorpe.* Wheaton, IL: Crossway, 1991.

Wayne, Israel. *Homeschooling from a Biblical Worldview.* Covert, MI: Wisdom's Gate, 2005.

Wilson, Douglas. *Excused Absence: Should Christian Kids Leave Public Schools?* Mission Viejo, CA: Crux, 2001.

Wilson, Douglas, ed. *The Case for Classical Christian Education.* Wheaton, IL: Crossway, 2003.

———. *The Paideia of God.* Moscow: Canon, 1999.

———. *Repairing the Ruins: The Classical & Christian Challenge to Modern Education.* Moscow: Canon, 1996.

"My wife and I homeschooled our two boys, and we would make the same decision again. Our reasons were basically the same ones that Adam Calvert enumerates in *Why We Homeschool*. It's good to have these reasons set forth cogently in a short book, and I recommend it to everyone who is thinking about this issue. Calvert sets forth powerfully the view that education is discipleship and therefore must be consistent with the Bible's worldview and with its Gospel."
—**John M. Frame,** Reformed Theological Seminary, Orlando, Florida

"Why do we do what we do? This is a question that those of us who take the task of discipling our children very seriously are often asked. Answering that question often turns on cultural, social, or moral concerns. But what this little book succeeds in doing is to steer the conversation to what the Scriptures affirm and confirm. Both practical and theological, both sobering and inspiring, this book is a welcome tool for families in this day of conflicting, polarizing worldviews."
—**George Grant,** Pastor of Parish Presbyterian Church

"This book is thought provoking and should be read by every parent, educator, and pastor. The content of this book must be at the center of our discussions about the nature, purpose, and goal in the biblically based education of our children. We might correctly state that there is no other foundation upon which we can educate our children than that of the Holy Scripture. The Bible is essential to our life, faith, and practice in all things."
—**Kenneth Gary Talbot,** President, Whitefield Theological Seminary and College

"Adam Calvert has written a fine, irenic introduction to Christian education designed to meet the objections of well-intentioned advocates of government education. This is a book you can put into the hands of friends honestly inquiring why a family would educate their children in a distinctly Christian way. I sincerely appreciate Adam's time and effort in producing this work."
—**P. Andrew Sandlin,** Founder & President, Center for Cultural Leadership

"This book is not about condemning the parent that chooses to send their children to the 'secular-humanist, state-sponsored' schools. It is about challenging the parent to consider a 'better way,' a way that permits both parent and child to pursue their faith and commitment to Christ primarily and to enfold the rest of their studies into that pursuit. It is a reasoned defense of—an apologia for—Christian Home-Schooling that Calvert has produced, and while he may not convince everyone of the model, he has provided a formidable argument that those who still choose a secular model cannot refute."
—**Win Groseclose,** The North American Reformed Seminary

"Adam Calvert succinctly but effectively canvases the oft asked question of homeschooling parents: Why do you homeschool? His well-reasoned and articulate answer without hesitance goes to the core of the issue: education is discipleship . . . This short but comprehensive explanation will serve the honest inquirer with 'fruit in due season' and, in the case of those already pursuing this most rewarding of family lifestyles, a more solid foundation for purposeful continuance."
—**Tim Yarbrough,** Tim teaches extensively in the home schooling community throughout his area with lectures and projects in economics, history and cultural reformation

"*Why We Homeschool* is an extremely helpful addition to the much-needed discussion on Christian education. The book looks at the question of schooling from a biblical and presuppositional perspective, and carefully and cleverly makes the case that God mandates Christian parents to give their covenant children a Christ centered education. This book has the potential to significantly help the church, and I strongly recommend it to any parent that I know."
—**Colin Gunn,** Co-Writer/Director/Producer, *IndoctriNation: Public Schools and the Decline of Christianity in America*

www.ingramcontent.com/pod-product-compliance
Lightning Source LLC
Chambersburg PA
CBHW070513090426
42735CB00012B/2764